The Forge

WHERE MEN ARE SHAPED FOR PURPOSE

Covenant Men in Leadership

The Forge
WHERE MEN ARE SHAPED FOR PURPOSE

Weekly Devotional

This is a nonfiction work. However, certain sections have been lightly fictionalized or dramatized for illustrative purposes. Any resemblance to actual persons, living or deceased, is purely coincidental.

Copyright © 2025 CP Carrington
all rights reserved
ISBN 979-8-9892386-9-9 (paperback edition)
Printed by Connect Books in the United States of America

**Connect Books
USA**

PO BOX 903 Wakefield VA. USA 23888
Connectbooks.pub

All rights reserved. No part of this book may be reproduced in any form or by an electronic or mechanical means, including information storage and retrieval systems, without permission in writing from the publisher, except by a reviewer who may quote brief passages in a review.

Scripture quotations are from the ESV® Bible (The Holy Bible, English Standard Version®), © 2001 by Crossway, a publishing ministry of Good News Publishers. Used by permission. All rights reserved. The ESV text may not be quoted in any publication made available to the public by a Creative Commons license. The ESV may not be translated in whole or in part into any other language.

Dedication

To Micheal and Cindy, Your unwavering dedication and quiet faithfulness have been a beacon of strength. The ministry God entrusted to you was unexpected and uninvited, but it was deeply needed. You answered His call with courage, and your obedience continues to inspire.

Contents

Welcome to The Forge 3

SECTION 1 9
Week 1. Yielding to God's Authority: 11
Week 2. Faithful Servanthood: 19
Week 3. Visionary Leadership: 25
Week 4. Integrity and Honesty: 33
Week 5. Courage in Adversity: 41
Week 6. Discipleship and Mentorship: 49
Week 7. Emotional Intelligence: 57
Week 8. Conflict Resolution: 65
" Week 9. Prayerful Leadership: 73

SECTION 2 81
Week 10. Financial Stewardship: 83
Week 11. Family as a Priority: 91
Week 12. Role of the Husband: 99
Week 13. Fatherhood and Guidance: 107
Week 14. Integrity in the Workplace: 115
Week 15. Community Engagement: 123

SECTION 3 131
Week 16. Witnessing and Evangelism: 133
Week 17. Accountability and Transparency: 141
Week 18. Patience and Understanding: 149

Week 19. Cultivating a Servant Heart: 157
Week 20. Moral and Ethical Leadership: 165

SECTION 4 173
Week 21. Raising Godly Children: 175
Week 22. Balancing Work and Family: 183
Week 23. Supportive Partnership in Marriage: 189
Week 24. Leadership in Worship: 197
Week 25. Overcoming Temptation: 205
Week 26. Fostering a Culture of Honor: 213
Week 27. Listening and Communication: 221
Week 28. Embracing Diversity: 229
Week 29. Service to the Vulnerable: 237
Week 30. Resilience in Leadership: 245

SECTION 5 253
Week 31. Building a Legacy of Faith: 255
Week 32. The Role of Humor and Joy: 263
Week 33. Gratitude and Contentment: 271
Week 34. Sabbath Rest: 279
Week 35. Social Responsibility: 287
Week 36. Intentionality in Relationships: 299
Week 37. Apologetics and Defense of Faith: 307
Week 38. Building Trust and Reliability: 315
Week 39. Endurance in Trials: 323
Week 40. Responding to Criticism: 331

SECTION 6 339
Week 41. Promoting Peace and Unity: 341
Week 42. Advocating for the Truth: 349
Week 43. Utilizing Spiritual Gifts: 357
Week 44. Healthy Boundaries: 365
Week 45. Living a Life of Worship: 373
Week 46. Supporting Church Leadership: 381
Week 47. Long term Vision: 389
Week 48. Empathy and Compassion: 397
Week 49. Promoting Lifelong Learning: 405
Week 50. Creating Safe Spaces: 413
Week 51. Navigating Change: 421
Week 52. Faithfulness in Small Things: 429
Leader's Addendum: 437

Men Leadership Devotional

Author's Note:
Back to the Anvil

As a Christian counselor, I have the privilege—and the burden—of sitting with hundreds of men, women, and couples every month. Over time, a theme has become heartbreakingly clear: men are struggling. They feel lost in today's culture, unsure of who they are or how to lead. Many carry deep shame. Others have simply given up, retreating into passivity or distraction. The culture mocks their masculinity, the church often doesn't know how to engage them, and the result is devastating: broken marriages, fatherless homes, isolated men, and discouraged women.

And it's not just the men who are suffering.

I've listened to countless women weep—not because they want to take the lead in their homes, but because they no longer trust the man in their life to do it with integrity, wisdom, or safety. They're not asking for dominance. They're longing for a man they can trust. A man they can follow without fear. A man who walks humbly with God and takes up the weight of leadership not for his own power, but for the good of those entrusted to his care.

That's why I wrote *The Forge*.

This is more than a devotional—it's a journey back to the anvil of God. It's for the man who knows something's missing. It's for the man who wants to lead but doesn't know how. It's for the man who's tired of pretending, tired

2 The Forge

of failing, tired of wondering if this is all there is. It's for the man who's ready to be reshaped.

The Forge is designed to rebuild biblical masculinity from the inside out. Week by week, it will take you through themes of character, calling, courage, conviction, stewardship, and brotherhood. You won't just read—you'll reflect, wrestle, and grow. It's not about becoming the man the world expects. It's about becoming the man God had in mind when He formed you.

If you stick with this journey, I believe God will meet you in it—not to scold you, but to shape you. Not to crush you, but to craft you. Because He's not done with you. Not even close.

So welcome to *The Forge*.
It's time to rise.

—Dr. Chuck Carrington

Men's Leadership Devotional 3

Welcome to The Forge

The Forge is a yearlong devotional journey crafted to shape Christian men into spiritually grounded, emotionally resilient, and mission-focused leaders. This is not a quick-fix series of lessons. It's a progressive formation process, where each phase builds on the last, guiding you from inward surrender to outward legacy.

You won't be rushed. You'll be refined. This isn't about performance—it's about transformation.

We begin with the inward work of character, then move into the outward work of stewardship and leadership. Along the way, we'll face the heat of conviction, the weight of responsibility, and the sharpening of brotherhood. Each week offers Scripture, reflection, and practical challenge to help you live as the man God is shaping you to be.

The Journey Ahead

This devotional is divided into **six thematic phases**—each one focusing on a distinct area of biblical manhood. These sections are marked by symbolic icons that reflect not just content, but the *kind of inner work* God is doing in that season. What follows is a preview of that journey, so

4 The Forge

you can begin with clarity, purpose, and a sense of momentum.

 Section 1: Forged by God – Building the Inner Man

Symbol: Anvil with Hammer
Why: Represents God's shaping of a man's heart through pressure, heat, and truth.
Weeks 1–9:

Spiritual Alignment: Yielding to God, Serving, Vision (Weeks 1–3)

Core Character: Integrity, Courage, Mentorship, Emotional Intelligence (Weeks 4–7)

Leadership in Relationship: Conflict Resolution, Prayerful Leadership (Weeks 8–9)

We begin at the anvil. Before you can lead others, you must be led by God. He doesn't just improve men—He *remakes* them. Here is where the hammer of God begins to fall.

 **Section 2: Stewards of Life – Managing What Matters**

Symbol: Tool Belt
Why: Signifies readiness to build, repair, and care for what God has entrusted.
Weeks 10–15:

Financial Stewardship (Week 10)

Family Leadership: Home, Husband, Father (Weeks 11–13)

Workplace and Community: Vocational Integrity, Civic Engagement (Weeks 14–15)

Leadership begins where you live. What God places in your hands—your relationships, work, and resources—He calls you to manage with wisdom and faithfulness.

 Section 3: Men on Mission – Courage, Conviction, and Calling

Symbol: Shield with Cross
Why: Emphasizes spiritual battle, direction, and moral clarity.
Weeks 16–20:

Evangelism (Week 16)

Accountability (Week 17)

Patience, Service, Ethics (Weeks 18–20)

A man on mission doesn't drift. He advances. These weeks will call you to live boldly, speak truth, and stand firm in a world that wants you to bend.

 Section 4: Living as Leaders – Impacting Family and Culture

Symbol: House with Light in the Window
Why: Represents influence that starts in the home and radiates outward.
Weeks 21–30:

Household Roles: Children, Balance, Marriage (Weeks 21–23)

Spiritual Disciplines: Worship, Temptation (Weeks 24–25)

Social Maturity: Honor, Communication, Diversity, Service, Resilience (Weeks 26–30)

6 The Forge

Your character is revealed in how you handle closeness. These reflections will shape how you lead, love, and live in your home and community.

Section 5: Legacy in the Making – Inner Life & Endurance

Symbol: Hourglass
Why: Symbolizes time, perseverance, and the kind of life that outlasts you.
Weeks 31–40:

Inner Life: Legacy, Joy, Gratitude (Weeks 31–33)

Sabbath and Justice (Weeks 34–35)

Long Obedience: Intentionality, Apologetics, Reliability, Endurance, Criticism (Weeks 36–40)

This phase slows the pace—but deepens the roots. You'll reflect on what kind of man you're becoming and what kind of legacy you're leaving.

Section 6: Leading Together – Spiritual Influence and Faithfulness

Symbol: Linked Chain
Why: Represents brotherhood, shared strength, and lasting influence.
Weeks 41–52:

Influence and Gifts: Unity, Truth, Spiritual Gifts (Weeks 41–43)

Sacred Leadership: Boundaries, Worship, Church Support (Weeks 44–46)

Legacy Roles: Vision, Compassion, Lifelong Learning (Weeks 47–49)

Men's Leadership Devotional 7

Finishing Well: Safe Culture, Navigating Change, Small Faithful Acts (Weeks 50–52)

We finish strong not by walking alone, but by linking arms with other men—brothers, mentors, and spiritual sons. Leadership is never solo. It's forged in community.

Now the path is in front of you.

Step into each week with openness, reflection, and a willingness to be changed. Whether you're just starting out or deep into your calling, *The Forge* will sharpen, challenge, and strengthen you.

Welcome to the fire. **Welcome to The Forge.**

SECTION 1

Forged by God: Building the Inner Man

(*Weeks 1–9*)

Before you can lead others, you have to let God lead you. That's where we begin—at the anvil of character. This first section of *The Forge* is about surrender, trust, and the deep, sometimes quiet work God does in the hidden places of a man's heart. Yielding to His authority, walking in integrity, managing our emotions, resolving conflict, and staying grounded in prayer—these aren't surface traits. They're the foundation of godly manhood.

These weeks will challenge you to stop faking strength and start forging it through submission, humility, and honest spiritual alignment. You're not just reading devotionals—you're letting the Master Craftsman shape the man beneath the surface.

Week 1
Yielding to God's Authority

Recognizing God's ultimate authority and submitting to His will in all areas of life.

In a bustling city, there lived a man named Michael, a devoted father and husband who struggled to balance his career aspirations with his faith. As he climbed the corporate ladder, the pressure to compromise his values grew. One evening, after a particularly challenging day at work, Michael sat in his car, feeling overwhelmed. He remembered the words from Proverbs 3:5-6: "Trust in the Lord with all your heart, and do not lean on your own understanding." He closed his eyes and prayed, seeking clarity and direction.

That night, Michael felt a nudge in his spirit—a call to yield to God's authority over his life. He opened his Bible and read James 4:7: "Submit yourselves therefore to God. Resist the devil, and he will flee from you." It struck him that to truly lead his family and set a good example, he needed to acknowledge God in every aspect of his life, especially his career choices.

The next day, Michael faced a critical decision at work—a promotion that required him to overlook unethical practices. Remembering his prayer, he took a deep breath and chose integrity over ambition. He spoke with his supervisor, expressing his concerns and declining the promotion. It was a hard decision, but he felt an

12 The Forge

overwhelming sense of peace, knowing he had submitted to God's authority.

Over time, Michael's choice became a testimony to his colleagues. Many began to seek his advice, and he found himself mentoring younger men on navigating faith in the workplace. As he yielded to God's will, he not only found clarity in his own path but also inspired others to trust in the Lord.

In submitting his heart and decisions to God, Michael discovered that true leadership stems from humility and integrity. He embraced God's authority, and as a result, he witnessed the transformative power of walking in faith, fulfilling the purpose God had set before him while bringing light into his workplace and home.

> Old Testament: Proverbs 3:5-6 "Trust in the Lord with all your heart, and do not lean on your own understanding. In all your ways acknowledge him, and he will make straight your paths."
>
> New Testament: James 4:7 "Submit yourselves therefore to God. Resist the devil, and he will flee from you."

As Christian men, yielding to God's authority is a cornerstone of our faith, guiding us in every aspect of our lives. Proverbs 3:5-6 urges us to trust in the Lord wholeheartedly, rather than relying on our limited understanding. When we acknowledge Him in all our ways, He promises to make our paths straight, leading us toward His perfect will. In James 4:7, we are reminded that submitting to God not only strengthens our relationship with Him but also equips us to resist temptation and the distractions of this world. Let us strive to embrace His authority with humility, seeking His guidance in our decisions and actions. As we submit our hearts and lives to Him, we can experience the peace and clarity that comes from walking in His light, confidently fulfilling the purpose He has set before us.

🛠 The Forge Weekly Reflection Sheet

Personal Study & Leadership Accountability Questions

1. Theme in My Life: This week's theme was
"____"

In my current life, I see this theme at work in the area of:
"____
__________________________________"

2. Key Verse Insight: The Scripture that stood out most to me this week was:
"____
__________________________________"

3. *Because it reminded/taught/convicted me that:*
"____
____
____
_____________________"

4. Connection—The story of ________ made me think about:
"____
__________________________________"

5. *A similar situation in my life has been:*
"____
____
____
_____________________"

16 The Forge

6. God's Prompting: One way I feel God is prompting me to grow or change this week is:

"_____
_____
_____
_____"

7. Action Step: As a man of faith and leadership, one practical step I will take this week is:

"_____
_____
_____
_____"

8. Prayer Focus: I sense the need to bring this to God in prayer:

"_____
_____
_____
_____"

9. *I also want to lift up these specific people or situations:*

"_____
_____
_____
_____"

10. Brotherhood Check-in:
One truth I need to share or process with another man is:

"_____
_____
_____
_____"

11. I plan to connect with: _____ by (day/time): _____

12. Refining at The Forge:
This week, God is shaping me most in the area of:
" _____
_____
_____
_____ "

13. I want to remain faithful in this process by:
" _____
_____
_____
_____ "

Week 2
Faithful Servanthood

Embracing the call to serve others selflessly, following Christ's example of humility.

John had always been a leader at work, praised for his strategic mind and decision-making skills. But as he sat in church one Sunday morning, listening to a sermon on servanthood, he felt a stirring in his heart. The pastor read from Isaiah 61:1, describing the call to bring good news to the poor and bind up the brokenhearted. John realized that while he was successful in his career, he had overlooked the deeper calling to serve others selflessly, just as Christ had done.

Later that week, John noticed an elderly neighbor, Mr. Thompson, struggling with his groceries. Normally, John would have waved and gone on his way, but this time he felt compelled to help. He offered to carry the bags inside, and as they walked, Mr. Thompson began to share about his recent loss of his wife and how lonely he had been. John listened intently, offering a kind word and a listening ear.

Inspired by Mark 10:45, where Jesus came not to be served but to serve, John started looking for more opportunities to serve quietly and humbly. He began volunteering at a local shelter, serving meals, and spending time with people who felt forgotten. At home, he was more attentive to his wife and children, focusing less on his own needs and more on how he could support and uplift them.

John's acts of service were small but impactful. Through each one, he felt a deeper connection to Christ's mission and a growing sense of purpose. He saw the joy in others' faces and realized that faithful servanthood wasn't about grand gestures but about simple, consistent acts of love. In embracing humility and selflessness, John became a vessel of Christ's grace, fostering hope and healing in his own community, one act of kindness at a time. Old Testament: Isaiah 61:1 "The Spirit of the Lord God is upon me, because the Lord has anointed me to bring good news to the poor; he has sent me to bind up the brokenhearted..."

New Testament: Mark 10:45 "For even the Son of Man came not to be served but to serve, and to give his life as a ransom for many."

As Christian men, we are called to embrace faithful servanthood, reflecting the humility and selflessness of Christ in our daily lives. Isaiah 61:1 reminds us of the anointing to bring good news to the marginalized and to heal the brokenhearted, echoing the heart of our Savior. In Mark 10:45, we see the ultimate example of service—Jesus, the Son of Man, who came not to be served but to serve, giving His life as a ransom for many. Let us follow in His footsteps by actively seeking ways to serve others, whether through acts of kindness, listening to those in need, or standing alongside the vulnerable. In doing so, we not only honor Christ but also become instruments of His love and grace in the world, fostering hope and healing in our communities.

Men's Leadership Devotional 21

⚒ The Forge Weekly Reflection Sheet

Personal Study & Leadership Accountability Questions

1. **Theme in My Life:** This week's theme was
"_____"
In my current life, I see this theme at work in the area of:
"_____
_____"

2. **Key Verse Insight:** The Scripture that stood out most to me this week was:
"_____
_____"

3. **Because it reminded/taught/convicted me that:**
"_____
_____
_____
_____"

4. **Connection—The story of _____ made me think about:**
"_____
_____"

5. *A similar situation in my life has been:*
"_____
_____
_____
_____"

22 The Forge

6. God's Prompting: One way I feel God is prompting me to grow or change this week is:

"_____
_____
_____
_____"

7. Action Step: As a man of faith and leadership, one practical step I will take this week is:

"_____
_____
_____
_____"

8. Prayer Focus: I sense the need to bring this to God in prayer:

"_____
_____
_____
_____"

9. *I also want to lift up these specific people or situations:*

"_____
_____
_____
_____"

10. Brotherhood Check-in:
One truth I need to share or process with another man is:

"_____
_____
_____
_____"

11. I plan to connect with: _____ **by (day/time):**
_____

12. Refining at The Forge:
This week, God is shaping me most in the area of:
"_____
_____
_____
_____"

13. *I want to remain faithful in this process by:*
"_____
_____
_____
_____"

Week 3
Visionary Leadership

Developing and communicating a clear vision rooted in God's Word for personal and communal goals.

David had always been active in his church, helping wherever needed, but he often felt there was something missing—a clear sense of direction, a purpose that went beyond his individual actions. One night, during his quiet time, he read Habakkuk 2:2: "Write the vision; make it plain on tablets, so he may run who reads it." The verse resonated deeply with him, prompting David to pause and reflect on the importance of having a clear vision, not just for his own life but for his family and his church community.

The following morning, David spent time in prayer, asking God to guide him in crafting a vision that reflected His will. Inspired by Acts 2:17, he felt called to bring his church's scattered efforts into alignment with a shared mission. He envisioned a community where everyone's gifts were recognized and utilized—a place where God's Spirit moved freely, empowering men and women to serve boldly.

David wrote down his thoughts, making the vision plain and actionable. He organized a meeting with the church leadership, presenting his ideas clearly: "We are a community empowered by God's Spirit, called to serve, uplift, and transform lives. Let's create a space where

26 The Forge

everyone, young and old, can prophesy, dream, and act on the vision God has placed in their hearts."

His passion was contagious. The elders and members of the church, who had often felt directionless, caught the vision. They started organizing specific ministries focused on outreach, discipleship, and community service, each guided by the common purpose David had articulated. Small groups flourished, and people felt inspired to contribute their gifts, whether through teaching, helping the needy, or simply praying for others.

As the church embraced this vision, it became more than just a congregation; it transformed into a beacon of hope in the community. David's decision to listen to God's call for visionary leadership brought clarity and direction, turning a collection of well-meaning efforts into a unified mission. His obedience to make the vision plain empowered others to run with it, fulfilling God's purpose and building a community that glorified Him.

> Old Testament: Habakkuk 2:2 "And the Lord answered me: 'Write the vision; make it plain on tablets, so he may run who reads it.'"
>
> New Testament: Acts 2:17 "And in the last days it shall be, God declares, that I will pour out my Spirit on all flesh, and your sons and your daughters shall prophesy..."

As Christian men, we are called to embrace visionary leadership, developing and communicating a clear vision rooted in God's Word for both our personal lives and our communities. Habakkuk 2:2 encourages us to write down the vision and make it plain, ensuring that it inspires and guides those who encounter it. This clarity allows us to lead with purpose and conviction, inviting others to join us in the journey of faith. In Acts 2:17, we are reminded that

Men's Leadership Devotional 27

God desires to pour out His Spirit upon all, empowering us to prophesy and share His message boldly. Let us seek His guidance through prayer and Scripture, crafting a vision that reflects His will and ignites passion within our hearts. By aligning our goals with His purpose, we can inspire others to run with us, fostering a community rooted in faith and driven by a shared mission for His glory.

Men's Leadership Devotional 29

⚒ The Forge Weekly Reflection Sheet

Personal Study & Leadership Accountability Questions

1. **Theme in My Life: This week's theme was**
   " _____ "
   In my current life, I see this theme at work in the area of:
   " _____
   _____ "

2. **Key Verse Insight: The Scripture that stood out most to me this week was:**
   " _____
   _____ "

3. **Because it reminded/taught/convicted me that:**
   " _____
   _____
   _____
   _____ "

4. **Connection—The story of _____ made me think about:**
   " _____
   _____ "

5. *A similar situation in my life has been:*
   " _____
   _____
   _____
   _____ "

6. **God's Prompting:** One way I feel God is prompting me to grow or change this week is:

   "_____
   _____
   _____
   _____"

7. **Action Step:** As a man of faith and leadership, one practical step I will take this week is:

   "_____
   _____
   _____
   _____"

8. **Prayer Focus:** I sense the need to bring this to God in prayer:

   "_____
   _____
   _____
   _____"

9. *I also want to lift up these specific people or situations:*

   "_____
   _____
   _____
   _____"

10. **Brotherhood Check-in:**
    One truth I need to share or process with another man is:

    "_____
    _____
    _____
    _____"

11. I plan to connect with: _____ by (day/time): _____

12. **Refining at The Forge:**
    This week, God is shaping me most in the area of:
    "_____
    _____
    _____
    _____"

13. *I want to remain faithful in this process by:*
    "_____
    _____
    _____
    _____"

Week 4
Integrity and Honesty

Leading with integrity, ensuring that actions align with biblical principles and truth.

Jacob was a respected manager at his company, known for his work ethic and leadership skills. However, he found himself facing a difficult decision when his supervisor, Mr. Hayes, asked him to adjust the sales reports to make the quarterly earnings look better than they actually were. "It's just a small change," Mr. Hayes insisted. "Everyone does it, and it will keep the shareholders happy."

Jacob felt the weight of the request immediately. He knew that altering the reports, even slightly, would compromise his integrity. Proverbs 10:9 echoed in his mind: "Whoever walks in integrity walks securely, but he who makes his ways crooked will be found out." He realized that cutting corners might provide short-term benefits, but it would ultimately lead him down a path of dishonesty.

That evening, Jacob prayed for wisdom, seeking guidance on how to handle the situation in a way that honored God. He was reminded of 2 Corinthians 8:21: "For we aim at what is honorable not only in the Lord's sight but also in the sight of man." Jacob knew that he needed to act in a way that reflected both his faith and his commitment to truth.

The next day, Jacob approached Mr. Hayes with a calm but firm resolve. "I understand the pressure to meet expectations, but I can't alter the reports. It wouldn't be right before God or our team. I believe we should find a solution that maintains our integrity." Mr. Hayes looked surprised, but after a moment of silence, he nodded. "I appreciate your honesty, Jacob. Let's find another way."

Jacob's refusal to compromise inspired his colleagues, who had often felt pressured to make similar unethical choices. His decision to stand firm on biblical principles not only protected his own integrity but also set a new standard for honesty within the company. Over time, Jacob's unwavering commitment to truth earned him greater trust and respect from his peers, demonstrating that leading with integrity isn't just about making the right choice in a moment—it's about building a legacy of honor.

Jacob's example reminded everyone that true leadership is about aligning actions with values, even when it's hard. By choosing integrity over convenience, he reflected Christ's character, showing that in a world full of shortcuts, walking securely in God's truth is the only path that truly leads to lasting success.

> Old Testament: Proverbs 10:9 "Whoever walks in integrity walks securely, but he who makes his ways crooked will be found out."
>
> New Testament: 2 Corinthians 8:21 "For we aim at what is honorable not only in the Lord's sight but also in the sight of man."

As Christian men, we are called to lead with integrity and honesty, allowing our actions to reflect the truth of God's Word. Proverbs 10:9 reminds us that those who walk in integrity walk securely, while those who choose a crooked path will ultimately be revealed. In 2 Corinthians 8:21, we are urged to aim for what is honorable, both in the Lord's sight and in the sight of others. Let us strive to align our lives with biblical principles, ensuring our words and actions match, for integrity is not just about personal conduct; it's about building trust and reflecting Christ's character in a world that often values expedience over truth. May we be men of integrity, standing firm in our commitment to honesty and honor, knowing that our faithful witness can lead others to experience the transformative power of God's love.

⚒ The Forge Weekly Reflection Sheet

Personal Study & Leadership Accountability Questions

1. **Theme in My Life:** This week's theme was
   "_____"
   In my current life, I see this theme at work in the area of:
   "_____
   _____"

2. **Key Verse Insight:** The Scripture that stood out most to me this week was:
   "_____
   _____"

3. **Because it reminded/taught/convicted me that:**
   "_____
   _____
   _____
   _____"

4. **Connection**—The story of _____ made me think about:
   "_____
   _____"

5. *A similar situation in my life has been:*
   "_____
   _____
   _____
   _____"

6. **God's Prompting: One way I feel God is prompting me to grow or change this week is:**
   "_____
   _____
   _____
   _____"

7. **Action Step: As a man of faith and leadership, one practical step I will take this week is:**
   "_____
   _____
   _____
   _____"

8. **Prayer Focus: I sense the need to bring this to God in prayer:**
   "_____
   _____
   _____
   _____"

9. *I also want to lift up these specific people or situations:*
   "_____
   _____
   _____
   _____"

10. **Brotherhood Check-in:**
    One truth I need to share or process with another man is:
    "_____
    _____
    _____
    _____"

11. I plan to connect with: _____ by (day/time): _____

12. Refining at The Forge:
    This week, God is shaping me most in the area of:
    "_____
    _____
    _____
    _____"

13. *I want to remain faithful in this process by:*
    "_____
    _____
    _____
    _____"

Week 5
Courage in Adversity

Standing firm in faith and taking bold actions, especially in challenging circumstances.

Anthony was a firefighter, used to facing danger, but nothing could have prepared him for the wildfire that tore through his community. The flames were intense, and the smoke thickened the air, making it difficult to see or breathe. As the captain of his team, he felt the weight of responsibility—every decision he made could mean the difference between life and death. That night, as the fire raged, Anthony found himself at a crossroads. The blaze was advancing quickly toward a neighborhood, and his team was exhausted, their fear palpable.

In the quiet of his heart, Anthony remembered the words of Joshua 1:9: "Be strong and courageous. Do not be frightened, and do not be dismayed, for the Lord your God is with you wherever you go." Those words had been his anchor throughout his life, but now, in the face of overwhelming danger, he had to put them into action.

Anthony called his team together. "We've trained for this moment," he said, trying to steady his voice. "We are not alone in this fight. God is with us, and we have everything we need to get through this." His calm but firm conviction bolstered the team's morale. They knew Anthony wasn't just spouting empty words; his faith was real, and it gave them courage to keep pushing forward.

42 The Forge

With renewed determination, Anthony led his team into the heart of the flames. The conditions were treacherous, and at times, fear threatened to creep in. But Anthony kept reminding himself of 2 Timothy 1:7: "For God gave us a spirit not of fear but of power and love and self-control." He focused on each task with a steady hand, trusting that God's strength would guide him through every challenge.

By the end of the night, Anthony and his team had successfully diverted the fire away from the homes, saving countless lives and properties. Exhausted but grateful, Anthony reflected on the day's events. He realized that courage wasn't the absence of fear—it was the willingness to act in spite of it, grounded in the assurance that God was with him every step of the way.

Anthony's bravery didn't just protect his community; it inspired his fellow firefighters and neighbors. They saw in him a man who trusted God in the face of adversity, who stood firm and took bold action when it mattered most. His courage became a living testimony of God's power and faithfulness, proving that when we lean on His strength, no challenge is too great.

> Old Testament: Joshua 1:9 "Have I not commanded you? Be strong and courageous. Do not be frightened, and do not be dismayed, for the Lord your God is with you wherever you go."

> New Testament: 2 Timothy 1:7 "For God gave us a spirit not of fear but of power and love and self-control."

As Christian men, we are called to exhibit courage in adversity, standing firm in our faith and taking bold actions even in the face of challenges. Joshua 1:9 commands us to be strong and courageous, reminding us that we are never alone—God goes with us wherever we venture. This assurance empowers us to confront our fears, knowing that His presence is our greatest strength. Similarly, 2 Timothy 1:7 tells us that God has given us a spirit not of fear, but of power, love, and self-control. Let us embrace this spirit as we navigate life's trials, leaning on His strength to guide us through uncertainty. By taking courageous steps, we not only honor God but also inspire those around us to trust in His faithfulness, transforming our adversity into a testimony of His grace and power.

Men's Leadership Devotional 45

⚒ The Forge Weekly Reflection Sheet

Personal Study & Leadership Accountability Questions

1. **Theme in My Life: This week's theme was**
   "_____"
   In my current life, I see this theme at work in the area of:
   "_____
   _____"

2. **Key Verse Insight: The Scripture that stood out most to me this week was:**
   "_____
   _____"

3. **Because it reminded/taught/convicted me that:**
   "_____
   _____
   _____
   _____"

4. **Connection—The story of _____ made me think about:**
   "_____
   _____"

5. *A similar situation in my life has been:*
   "_____
   _____
   _____
   _____"

46 The Forge

6. **God's Prompting: One way I feel God is prompting me to grow or change this week is:**
   "_____
   _____
   _____
   _____"

7. **Action Step: As a man of faith and leadership, one practical step I will take this week is:**
   "_____
   _____
   _____
   _____"

8. **Prayer Focus: I sense the need to bring this to God in prayer:**
   "_____
   _____
   _____
   _____"

9. *I also want to lift up these specific people or situations:*
   "_____
   _____
   _____
   _____"

10. **Brotherhood Check-in:**
    One truth I need to share or process with another man is:
    "_____
    _____
    _____
    _____"

11. I plan to connect with: _____ by (day/time): _____

12. Refining at The Forge:
    This week, God is shaping me most in the area of:
    "_____
    _____
    _____
    _____"

13. *I want to remain faithful in this process by:*
    "_____
    _____
    _____
    _____"

Week 6
Discipleship and Mentorship

Actively engaging in mentoring relationships to guide others in their spiritual journeys.

When Robert was a young man, his mentor, Pastor James, invested countless hours teaching him the Scriptures, sharing wisdom, and encouraging him through life's ups and downs. Now, years later, Robert felt called to pass on the same kind of guidance to others. He saw the potential in a young man named Chris, who had recently started attending his church. Chris was eager to grow in his faith but lacked direction and confidence in navigating his spiritual journey.

One Sunday after church, Robert approached Chris and invited him to coffee. As they sat down, Robert shared his story, including how Pastor James had shaped his life through mentorship. "I wouldn't be where I am today without someone investing in me," Robert said. "I see that same potential in you, Chris. How would you feel about meeting regularly to study the Word and talk about life?"

Chris was excited and agreed. Over the next few months, they met every week, diving into Scripture and discussing everything from work challenges to personal struggles. Robert didn't just teach Chris; he listened, asked questions, and allowed Chris to share his insights, understanding that true discipleship was about mutual sharpening, as Proverbs 27:17 describes: "Iron sharpens iron, and one man sharpens another."

50 The Forge

One day, during a conversation about 2 Timothy 2:2, Robert encouraged Chris to start thinking about who he could mentor in the future. "Discipleship isn't just about what we learn—it's about passing it on," Robert explained. "Paul's words remind us to entrust what we've learned to faithful men who can teach others. You have something valuable to give."

Inspired, Chris began to notice younger guys at church who reminded him of himself a year ago—full of questions, searching for guidance. He took the leap and started mentoring a teenager named Luke, meeting with him to study the Bible and talk about faith. The mentorship, initially intimidating for Chris, quickly became a source of joy as he saw Luke grow in confidence and understanding.

As Robert watched Chris take on the mantle of mentorship, he saw the beauty of discipleship come full circle. It wasn't just about Robert pouring into Chris; it was about creating a ripple effect that extended beyond them both. Each meeting, each conversation was a link in a chain that strengthened their community, drawing people closer to Christ.

Through their relationship, Robert and Chris discovered the true power of Proverbs 27:17 and 2 Timothy 2:2. Discipleship was not just a command but a lifeline—an opportunity to build each other up and guide the next generation in faith. In investing in others, they were not just growing individually but cultivating a thriving community rooted in love, wisdom, and God's Word.

> Old Testament: Proverbs 27:17 "Iron sharpens iron, and one man sharpens another."

> New Testament: 2 Timothy 2:2 "And what you have heard from me in the presence of many witnesses

entrust to faithful men, who will be able to teach others also."

As Christian men, we are called to engage in discipleship and mentorship, recognizing the vital role we play in guiding others on their spiritual journeys. Proverbs 27:17 reminds us that "iron sharpens iron," emphasizing the importance of mutual growth and accountability in our relationships. In 2 Timothy 2:2, Paul encourages us to entrust what we have learned to faithful men, who will then teach others, creating a chain of discipleship that strengthens the body of Christ. Let us actively seek out opportunities to mentor those around us, sharing our experiences and wisdom while also being open to learning from them. By investing in these relationships, we not only fulfill Christ's commission to make disciples but also cultivate a community rooted in faith and love, empowering others to grow closer to God and fulfill their own calling.

Men's Leadership Devotional 53

✼ The Forge Weekly Reflection Sheet

Personal Study & Leadership Accountability Questions

1. **Theme in My Life: This week's theme was**
   "_____"
   In my current life, I see this theme at work in the area of:
   "_____
   _____"

2. **Key Verse Insight: The Scripture that stood out most to me this week was:**
   "_____
   _____"

3. ***Because it reminded/taught/convicted me that:***
   "_____
   _____
   _____
   _____"

4. **Connection—The story of _____ made me think about:**
   "_____
   _____"

5. ***A similar situation in my life has been:***
   "_____
   _____
   _____
   _____"

6. **God's Prompting:** One way I feel God is prompting me to grow or change this week is:

   "_____
   _____
   _____
   _____ "

7. **Action Step:** As a man of faith and leadership, one practical step I will take this week is:

   "_____
   _____
   _____
   _____ "

8. **Prayer Focus:** I sense the need to bring this to God in prayer:

   "_____
   _____
   _____
   _____ "

9. *I also want to lift up these specific people or situations:*

   "_____
   _____
   _____
   _____ "

10. **Brotherhood Check-in:**
    One truth I need to share or process with another man is:

    "_____
    _____
    _____
    _____ "

11. I plan to connect with: _____ by (day/time): _____

12. Refining at The Forge:
    This week, God is shaping me most in the area of:
    "_____
    _____
    _____
    _____"

13. *I want to remain faithful in this process by:*
    "_____
    _____
    _____
    _____"

Week 7
Emotional Intelligence

Cultivating the ability to understand and manage emotions, fostering healthy relationships.

William sat at the dinner table, his mind still reeling from a tough day at work. As the conversation with his wife, Sarah, shifted to the children's behavior, frustration began to simmer. Their teenage son, Ethan, had been acting out lately, and William's patience was wearing thin.

"Ethan needs to learn some respect," William snapped, his voice laced with anger. Sarah, sensing the tension, gently responded, "I know you're upset, but yelling won't help him listen. Let's talk about how we can approach this differently."

William took a deep breath, recalling Proverbs 15:1: "A soft answer turns away wrath, but a harsh word stirs up anger." He realized his words were adding fuel to the fire instead of bringing calm. In that moment, William paused, allowing Philippians 4:5 to guide him: "Let your reasonableness be known to everyone. The Lord is at hand."

He looked at Sarah, softened his tone, and said, "You're right. I've been letting my anger control me. Let's figure out a way to connect with Ethan instead of pushing him away."

Together, they brainstormed a plan to approach Ethan with understanding rather than confrontation. That evening,

58 The Forge

William sat down with his son, his voice calm and steady. "I know things have been tough, and I've been hard on you. I'm here to listen and work through this with you."

Ethan's guarded expression melted into a look of relief. Instead of another argument, they had a heartfelt conversation that opened doors to healing and connection.

Through this experience, William learned that cultivating emotional intelligence—understanding and managing his emotions—allowed him to lead his family with grace. By choosing a soft answer and showing reasonableness, he created an atmosphere of trust and respect, reflecting Christ's love in his home.

> Old Testament: Proverbs 15:1 "A soft answer turns away wrath, but a harsh word stirs up anger."
>
> New Testament: Philippians 4:5 "Let your reasonableness be known to everyone. The Lord is at hand."

As Christian men, cultivating emotional intelligence is essential for fostering healthy relationships and reflecting Christ's love in our interactions. Proverbs 15:1 teaches us that a soft answer can turn away wrath, highlighting the power of our words to diffuse tension and build bridges rather than walls. In Philippians 4:5, we are encouraged to let our reasonableness be evident to all, reminding us that our demeanor can draw others closer to God. By being mindful of our emotions and the emotions of those around us, we can respond with grace and understanding, creating an atmosphere of trust and respect. Let us commit to developing this vital skill, recognizing that as we manage our emotions and communicate with kindness, we not only honor God but also cultivate relationships that reflect His heart. May our lives be a testament to the peace and love of Christ, inviting others into deeper connection and understanding.

Men's Leadership Devotional 61

⚒ The Forge Weekly Reflection Sheet

Personal Study & Leadership Accountability Questions

1. **Theme in My Life: This week's theme was**
   "_____"

   In my current life, I see this theme at work in the area of:
   "_____
   _____"

2. **Key Verse Insight: The Scripture that stood out most to me this week was:**
   "_____
   _____"

3. **Because it reminded/taught/convicted me that:**
   "_____
   _____
   _____"

4. **Connection—The story of _____ made me think about:**
   "_____
   _____"

5. **A similar situation in my life has been:**
   "_____
   _____
   _____"

6. **God's Prompting:** One way I feel God is prompting me to grow or change this week is:
   "_____
   _____
   _____
   _____"

7. **Action Step:** As a man of faith and leadership, one practical step I will take this week is:
   "_____
   _____
   _____
   _____"

8. **Prayer Focus:** I sense the need to bring this to God in prayer:
   "_____
   _____
   _____
   _____"

9. *I also want to lift up these specific people or situations:*
   "_____
   _____
   _____
   _____"

10. **Brotherhood Check-in:**
    One truth I need to share or process with another man is:
    "_____
    _____
    _____
    _____"

11. I plan to connect with: _____ by (day/time): _____

12. Refining at The Forge:
    This week, God is shaping me most in the area of:
    "_____
    _____
    _____
    _____"

13. *I want to remain faithful in this process by:*
    "_____
    _____
    _____
    _____"

Men's Leadership Devotional 65

Week 8
Conflict Resolution

Navigating conflicts with wisdom and grace, promoting reconciliation and unity.

Mark had always prided himself on being the head of his household, but lately, things had been tense. His business was struggling, and the weight of financial stress had made him quick to anger. One evening, after a long day at work, Mark came home to find his teenage daughter, Emma, arguing with his wife, Lisa, about her curfew. The frustration bubbling inside him was about to boil over.

"Enough!" Mark shouted, his voice echoing through the house. Emma stormed off to her room, slamming the door, while Lisa stood there, hurt and disappointed. Mark's outburst had only deepened the divide.

Mark retreated to the kitchen, his heart heavy. As he sat alone, Proverbs 15:18 came to mind: "A hot-tempered man stirs up strife, but he who is slow to anger quiets contention." He realized his anger was not solving the problem but creating more strife. He knew that God called him to be a peacemaker, as Matthew 5:9 reminded him: "Blessed are the peacemakers, for they shall be called sons of God."

Determined to make things right, Mark took a deep breath, praying for wisdom and grace. He knocked on Emma's door and gently asked if they could talk. Sitting down together, Mark admitted, "I shouldn't have yelled. I let my frustration get the best of me, and I'm sorry. I want us to work through this as a family, with respect and understanding."

Emma, surprised by her father's humility, softened. They discussed her concerns and agreed on a plan that honored her growing independence while respecting family rules. Mark then spoke with Lisa, acknowledging his part in the conflict and asking for forgiveness.

By addressing the situation with a calm heart and a desire for peace, Mark began to heal the wounds caused by his anger. Through this experience, he learned that conflict resolution wasn't about winning an argument but about promoting reconciliation and unity.

Mark's decision to be a peacemaker that night not only brought healing to his family but also reflected the heart of God. His actions stood as a testament to the power of wisdom and grace in navigating conflicts, creating a home where love could thrive.

> Old Testament: Proverbs 15:18 "A hot tempered man stirs up strife, but he who is slow to anger quiets contention."
>
> New Testament: Matthew 5:9 "Blessed are the peacemakers, for they shall be called sons of God."

In our journey as Christian men, we are often faced with conflicts that test our patience and character. Proverbs 15:18 reminds us that a hot-tempered man only stirs up strife, while the wise man, who is slow to anger, brings calm to contentious situations. This call to measured response is echoed in Matthew 5:9, where we are blessed as peacemakers, reflecting the heart of our Father. Let us seek to navigate conflicts with wisdom and grace, promoting reconciliation and unity in all our relationships. By embodying these truths, we not only honor God but also foster an environment where His love can thrive, bringing healing to ourselves and others. May we strive to be men who actively pursue peace, standing firm in faith and extending grace even in the heat of disagreement.

Men's Leadership Devotional 69

⚒ The Forge Weekly Reflection Sheet

Personal Study & Leadership Accountability Questions

1. **Theme in My Life: This week's theme was**
   "_____"
   In my current life, I see this theme at work in the area of:
   "_____
   _____"

2. **Key Verse Insight: The Scripture that stood out most to me this week was:**
   "_____
   _____"

3. *Because it reminded/taught/convicted me that:*
   "_____
   _____
   _____
   _____"

4. **Connection—The story of _____ made me think about:**
   "_____
   _____"

5. *A similar situation in my life has been:*
   "_____
   _____
   _____"

6. **God's Prompting: One way I feel God is prompting me to grow or change this week is:**
   "_____
   _____
   _____
   _____"

7. **Action Step: As a man of faith and leadership, one practical step I will take this week is:**
   "_____
   _____
   _____
   _____"

8. **Prayer Focus: I sense the need to bring this to God in prayer:**
   "_____
   _____
   _____
   _____"

9. *I also want to lift up these specific people or situations:*
   "_____
   _____
   _____
   _____"

10. **Brotherhood Check-in:**
    One truth I need to share or process with another man is:
    "_____
    _____
    _____
    _____"

11. I plan to connect with: _____ by (day/time): _____

12. Refining at The Forge:
    This week, God is shaping me most in the area of:
    " _____
    _____
    _____
    _____ "

13. *I want to remain faithful in this process by:*
    " _____
    _____
    _____
    _____ "

Week 9
Prayerful Leadership

Prioritizing prayer in decision making and leadership, seeking God's guidance and wisdom.

Richard, a small business owner and church elder, was facing a crossroads. His company was struggling financially, and he was under pressure to make quick decisions that could impact his employees and family. With a critical meeting with his business partners approaching, Richard felt the weight of responsibility pressing heavily on his shoulders. Anxiety crept in, whispering fears of failure and uncertainty.

Late one evening, Richard sat at his desk, staring at spreadsheets filled with red numbers. The room was quiet, but his mind was loud with questions and doubts. It was then that 1 Chronicles 16:11 came to mind: "Seek the Lord and his strength; seek his presence continually!" Richard realized he had been relying solely on his own understanding and not inviting God into the process.

Instead of rushing into decisions, Richard closed his laptop, knelt by his chair, and prayed. "Lord, I need Your wisdom. Guide me in the decisions I must make. I lay my worries at Your feet, trusting that You are in control." He remembered Philippians 4:6-7: "Do not be anxious about anything, but in everything by prayer and supplication with thanksgiving let your requests be made known to God."

74 The Forge

As Richard prayed, he felt a peace that had been missing—the kind of peace that only comes from surrendering control to God. He asked for guidance not just for his business, but for his role as a leader, a husband, and a father. Richard's prayer wasn't just about solving problems; it was about aligning his heart with God's will.

The next day, Richard met with his partners with a renewed sense of calm. He shared his concerns but also his commitment to seeking God's guidance in every step. His honesty and reliance on prayer inspired his partners, who agreed to join him in prayer before making any major decisions.

Over the coming weeks, the business began to turn around—not just because of new strategies, but because Richard had shifted from anxious striving to prayerful leadership. He continued to seek God's presence daily, bringing every concern and decision before Him with thanksgiving.

Richard's leadership became a testimony to those around him. By prioritizing prayer, he demonstrated that true strength and wisdom come from God. His business flourished, but more importantly, Richard's heart and leadership reflected a deep trust in God's plan, creating an atmosphere of hope and faith among those he led.

Through prayerful leadership, Richard learned that the greatest decisions are made not in the boardroom, but on his knees. He found that by seeking God first, he was equipped to lead with wisdom, grace, and the peace that surpasses all understanding.

>Old Testament: 1 Chronicles 16:11 "Seek the Lord and his strength; seek his presence continually!"

Men's Leadership Devotional

New Testament: Philippians 4:6 7 "Do not be anxious about anything, but in everything by prayer and supplication with thanksgiving let your requests be made known to God."

As Christian men called to lead, we must prioritize prayer in every decision we face, recognizing that true strength comes from seeking the Lord. 1 Chronicles 16:11 reminds us to seek His presence continually, inviting His wisdom and guidance into our lives and leadership. In Philippians 4:6-7, we are encouraged not to be anxious but to bring everything before God in prayer, trusting that His peace will guard our hearts and minds. Let us embrace prayerful leadership, dedicating our decisions to God with thanksgiving and humility. By doing so, we align ourselves with His purpose, ensuring that our leadership reflects His love and wisdom, and fosters an atmosphere of trust and hope among those we lead. May we commit to seeking His presence daily, confident that in Him, we find the strength to lead well.

🛠 The Forge Weekly Reflection Sheet

Personal Study & Leadership Accountability Questions

1. Theme in My Life: This week's theme was
   "____"

   In my current life, I see this theme at work in the area of:
   "____
   ____"

2. Key Verse Insight: The Scripture that stood out most to me this week was:
   "____
   ____"

3. *Because it reminded/taught/convicted me that:*
   "____
   ____
   ____
   ____"

4. Connection—The story of ________ made me think about:
   "____
   ____"

5. *A similar situation in my life has been:*
   "____
   ____
   ____
   ____"

6. **God's Prompting: One way I feel God is prompting me to grow or change this week is:**
   "_____
   _____
   _____
   _____"

7. **Action Step: As a man of faith and leadership, one practical step I will take this week is:**
   "_____
   _____
   _____
   _____"

8. **Prayer Focus: I sense the need to bring this to God in prayer:**
   "_____
   _____
   _____
   _____"

9. *I also want to lift up these specific people or situations:*
   "_____
   _____
   _____
   _____"

10. **Brotherhood Check-in:**
    One truth I need to share or process with another man is:
    "_____
    _____
    _____
    _____"

11. I plan to connect with: _____ by (day/time): _____

12. **Refining at The Forge:**
    This week, God is shaping me most in the area of:
    "_____
    _____
    _____
    _____"

13. *I want to remain faithful in this process by:*
    "_____
    _____
    _____
    _____"

SECTION 2

Stewards of Life: Managing What Matters

(*Weeks 10–15*)

God doesn't just give us responsibilities—He entrusts them. Our families, finances, workplaces, and communities are not just burdens to manage, but sacred callings to steward. This section focuses on the practical arenas where a man's leadership is tested daily. Will we lead our homes with love? Will we handle our money with integrity? Will we show up where it counts, not just where it's convenient?

Here's where your theology meets your Tuesday afternoon. You'll be invited to recalibrate your priorities, invest more deeply in those closest to you, and live your life with intentional care and visible witness.

Week 10
Financial Stewardship

Managing resources wisely, demonstrating biblical principles of generosity and responsibility.

A Lesson in Financial Stewardship

Tom had always been a hard worker, climbing the corporate ladder and achieving a level of financial success he had dreamed of for years. With a beautiful home, luxury car, and an overflowing bank account, Tom seemed to have it all. Yet, despite his wealth, he often felt an emptiness that his possessions couldn't fill.

One evening, Tom was reviewing his finances, planning his next big investment, when his young son, Luke, came into the room holding a jar filled with coins. "Dad, I want to save this for kids who don't have food," Luke said earnestly. Tom was taken aback by his son's simple yet profound generosity.

Tom's mind flashed to Proverbs 21:20: "Precious treasure and oil are in a wise man's dwelling, but a foolish man devours it." He realized that while he had accumulated wealth, he had been consuming it on himself, neglecting the opportunity to use his resources for something greater. His priorities had been centered on comfort and status rather than stewardship.

Convicted, Tom spent time in prayer, asking God to guide him in how to use his resources wisely. He remembered 1

84 The Forge

Timothy 6:17-19: "As for the rich in this present age, charge them not to be haughty, nor to set their hopes on the uncertainty of riches..." Tom knew that his security was not in his bank account but in God, who had blessed him abundantly.

Inspired by his son's heart and his renewed sense of purpose, Tom began to re-evaluate his financial decisions. He started setting aside a portion of his income each month for charitable giving, supporting his church, and helping those in need. He also involved his family in these decisions, teaching his children the value of generosity and stewardship.

One Sunday, Tom shared with his small group how God had transformed his view of money. "It's not just about what we have; it's about how we use it," he said. "God has given us so much, and I want to honor Him by giving back."

Tom's commitment to financial stewardship extended beyond just writing checks. He volunteered his time, offered his business skills to help local non-profits, and began mentoring young men on how to manage their resources wisely. His life became a living example of God's call to generosity and responsibility.

Through this journey, Tom discovered that true fulfillment came not from accumulating wealth but from using it to bless others and advance God's kingdom. He learned that being a wise steward meant valuing what God had entrusted to him and investing it in eternal things.

Tom's transformation in financial stewardship showed his family and community that his hope was not in the uncertainty of riches but in the unfailing provision of God. His actions echoed a deeper trust, fostering a spirit of gratitude and generosity that reflected the heart of Christ.

Old Testament: Proverbs 21:20 "Precious treasure and oil are in a wise man's dwelling, but a foolish man devours it."

New Testament: 1 Timothy 6:17 19 "As for the rich in this present age, charge them not to be haughty, nor to set their hopes on the uncertainty of riches..."

As Christian men, we are called to practice financial stewardship, managing our resources wisely in accordance with biblical principles. Proverbs 21:20 teaches us that a wise man values his treasures, ensuring they are used for greater purposes, while the foolish man squanders what he has. In 1 Timothy 6:17-19, we are reminded not to place our hopes in the fleeting nature of wealth, but rather to use our resources generously and responsibly, storing up treasures in heaven. By embracing a mindset of stewardship, we honor God with our finances, reflecting His generosity and care for others. Let us commit to being intentional in our financial decisions, seeking ways to bless those around us and support the work of His kingdom. May our actions demonstrate that our trust is not in riches, but in the One who provides for all our needs, fostering a spirit of gratitude and generosity in our lives.

Men's Leadership Devotional 87

⚒ The Forge Weekly Reflection Sheet

Personal Study & Leadership Accountability Questions

1. **Theme in My Life: This week's theme was**
   " _____ "
   In my current life, I see this theme at work in the area of:
   " _____
   _____ "

2. **Key Verse Insight: The Scripture that stood out most to me this week was:**
   " _____
   _____ "

3. *Because it reminded/taught/convicted me that:*
   " _____
   _____
   _____
   _____ "

4. **Connection—The story of _____ made me think about:**
   " _____
   _____ "

5. *A similar situation in my life has been:*
   " _____
   _____
   _____
   _____ "

6. **God's Prompting: One way I feel God is prompting me to grow or change this week is:**

   "_____
   _____
   _____
   _____"

7. **Action Step: As a man of faith and leadership, one practical step I will take this week is:**

   "_____
   _____
   _____
   _____"

8. **Prayer Focus: I sense the need to bring this to God in prayer:**

   "_____
   _____
   _____
   _____"

9. *I also want to lift up these specific people or situations:*

   "_____
   _____
   _____
   _____"

10. **Brotherhood Check-in:**
    One truth I need to share or process with another man is:

    "_____
    _____
    _____
    _____"

11. I plan to connect with: _____ by (day/time): _____

12. Refining at The Forge:
This week, God is shaping me most in the area of:
"_____
_____
_____
_____"

13. *I want to remain faithful in this process by:*
"_____
_____
_____
_____"

Men's Leadership Devotional 91

Week 11
Family as a Priority

Leading with love and commitment within the family unit, nurturing spiritual growth.

A Father's Commitment to Family

Joseph was a successful project manager, known for his leadership and dedication at work. However, as his responsibilities grew, so did the hours he spent away from home. His wife, Anna, and their two children, Jake and Emma, often found themselves eating dinner without him. One night, as Joseph rushed out the door for yet another late meeting, Jake's small voice stopped him. "Dad, are you coming to my game tomorrow?"

Joseph hesitated, caught between his work demands and his son's hopeful eyes. He promised he'd try, but as he drove away, guilt settled in. That night, he couldn't shake the feeling that he was missing something far more important than a meeting.

The next morning, Joseph read his Bible, and Deuteronomy 6:6-7 resonated deeply: "And these words that I command you today shall be on your heart. You shall teach them diligently to your children…" Joseph realized he had been neglecting his primary role as a spiritual leader at home. He was providing financially, but his presence and guidance were lacking. Ephesians 6:4 echoed in his heart: "Fathers, do not provoke your children to anger, but bring them up in the discipline and instruction of the Lord." He knew that his absence was quietly frustrating his family, and he needed to change.

Determined to prioritize his family, Joseph rearranged his schedule, declining unnecessary meetings and making space for what truly mattered. That afternoon, he surprised Jake by showing up at his soccer game, cheering louder than anyone else on the sidelines. The joy on Jake's face reminded Joseph of the impact of simply being there.

Later that evening, Joseph gathered his family in the living room. He apologized for being distant and shared his desire to be more present and intentional. "I want us to grow together, not just as a family, but in our faith," he said. They decided to start a nightly family devotion, reading Scripture together and discussing how it applied to their lives.

As the weeks went by, these times became the highlight of their days. Joseph began teaching Jake and Emma about God's love, patience, and the importance of prayer, making the Word of God an integral part of their family life. He also made sure to nurture his relationship with Anna, spending time with her, listening, and praying together.

One night, as Joseph tucked Emma into bed, she hugged him tightly and whispered, "I love that you're home, Daddy." Her simple words affirmed that Joseph's decision to prioritize his family was the right one.

Through his renewed commitment, Joseph discovered that leading his family with love and dedication brought more fulfillment than any professional success. By teaching his children God's Word and nurturing their spiritual growth, he was laying a foundation of faith that would guide them for the rest of their lives.

Joseph's journey illustrated that true leadership begins at home. By prioritizing his family, he not only honored God but also created an environment where love, faith, and spiritual growth could thrive. His legacy would be one of a father who led with grace, commitment, and an unwavering dedication to his family's walk with the Lord.

> Old Testament: Deuteronomy 6:6 7 "And these words that I command you today shall be on your heart. You shall teach them diligently to your children..."
>
> New Testament: Ephesians 6:4 "Fathers, do not provoke your children to anger, but bring them up in the discipline and instruction of the Lord."

As Christian men, we are called to prioritize our families, leading with love and commitment to nurture their spiritual growth. Deuteronomy 6:6-7 reminds us that God's words should dwell in our hearts, prompting us to diligently teach them to our children, ensuring they understand His truths and love. In Ephesians 6:4, we are instructed to raise our children in the discipline and instruction of the Lord, doing so with patience and kindness rather than provoking them to anger. By making our families a priority, we create a foundation of faith and trust, guiding them toward a deeper relationship with God. Let us embrace this sacred responsibility, being present and intentional in our parenting and relationships, fostering an environment where spiritual growth can flourish. May our commitment to our families reflect Christ's love, enabling us to lead them with grace and purpose as we walk together in faith.

🛠 The Forge Weekly Reflection Sheet

Personal Study & Leadership Accountability Questions

1. Theme in My Life: This week's theme was
   "____"
   In my current life, I see this theme at work in the area of:
   "____
   ____"

2. Key Verse Insight: The Scripture that stood out most to me this week was:
   "____
   ____"

3. *Because it reminded/taught/convicted me that:*
   "____
   ____
   ____
   ____"

4. Connection—The story of __________ made me think about:
   "____
   ____"

5. *A similar situation in my life has been:*
   "____
   ____
   ____
   ____"

6. **God's Prompting:** One way I feel God is prompting me to grow or change this week is:
   "_____
   _____
   _____
   _____"

7. **Action Step:** As a man of faith and leadership, one practical step I will take this week is:
   "_____
   _____
   _____
   _____"

8. **Prayer Focus:** I sense the need to bring this to God in prayer:
   "_____
   _____
   _____
   _____"

9. *I also want to lift up these specific people or situations:*
   "_____
   _____
   _____
   _____"

10. **Brotherhood Check-in:**
    One truth I need to share or process with another man is:
    "_____
    _____
    _____
    _____"

11. I plan to connect with: _____ by (day/time): _____

12. Refining at The Forge:
    This week, God is shaping me most in the area of:
    "_____
    _____
    _____
    _____"

13. *I want to remain faithful in this process by:*
    "_____
    _____
    _____
    _____"

Week 12
Role of the Husband

Understanding and fulfilling the biblical role of loving and leading one's wife.

Embracing the Role of a Husband

James had been married to Lisa for nearly fifteen years. Their life was filled with the busyness of work, raising children, and managing the day-to-day challenges of family life. But lately, Lisa had seemed distant, and James often found himself frustrated, feeling unappreciated and misunderstood. One evening, after a particularly tense argument about finances, Lisa walked away in tears, leaving James alone with his thoughts.

Sitting in the quiet of their living room, James felt the weight of the distance growing between them. He picked up his Bible, hoping for comfort, and his eyes fell on Malachi 2:14: "But you say, 'Why does he not?' Because the Lord was witness between you and the wife of your youth, to whom you have been faithless…" James realized that while he hadn't physically betrayed Lisa, he had been unfaithful in other ways—neglecting her emotional needs, failing to cherish her, and taking her for granted.

As he continued reading, Ephesians 5:25 struck him deeply: "Husbands, love your wives, as Christ loved the church and gave himself up for her." James knew he had been far from this standard. Christ's love for the church was selfless, sacrificial, and unending—a stark contrast to his recent behavior.

Convicted, James went to find Lisa, who was sitting quietly in their bedroom. He sat beside her, taking her hand. "I'm sorry," he said, his voice filled with sincerity. "I've been so focused on my own frustrations that I've forgotten how to love you like Christ loves the church. I haven't been leading well, and I want to change that."

Over the next few weeks, James made intentional efforts to reconnect with Lisa. He began setting aside time each day to listen to her, not just to respond but to understand her heart. He started praying with her each morning, lifting up their marriage and asking God to guide him in loving her better.

James also took on more responsibilities around the house, easing Lisa's burden, and surprised her with thoughtful gestures that reminded her of their early years together. He encouraged her spiritual growth, supporting her dreams and involving her in decisions. He no longer saw his role as merely providing but as leading with love, humility, and respect.

One evening, as they shared a quiet dinner, Lisa looked at James and said, "I feel like I'm seeing the man I married again. Thank you for choosing us." Her words reaffirmed the impact of his commitment to living out his role as a husband according to God's design.

Through this journey, James learned that fulfilling his biblical role wasn't about demanding respect or being in control; it was about serving his wife with the same grace, patience, and selflessness that Christ showed the church. He realized that his love and leadership were not just responsibilities but privileges that honored God and nurtured their marriage.

James' transformation reflected the beauty of a husband who loves sacrificially, leading his wife with a heart full of Christ's love. By embracing his role, he built a marriage rooted in mutual respect, trust, and unwavering love, creating a home that honored God and reflected His purpose.

> Old Testament: Malachi 2:14 "But you say, 'Why does he not?' Because the Lord was witness between you and the wife of your youth, to whom you have been faithless..."
>
> New Testament: Ephesians 5:25 "Husbands, love your wives, as Christ loved the church and gave himself up for her."

As Christian men, understanding and fulfilling our role as husbands is a sacred calling that demands both love and commitment. Malachi 2:14 reminds us of the seriousness of our covenant, emphasizing that the Lord witnesses our faithfulness to our wives. In Ephesians 5:25, we are called to love our wives as Christ loved the church, which means sacrificially and unconditionally. This love goes beyond mere affection; it involves leading with humility, serving wholeheartedly, and nurturing her spiritual and emotional well-being. Let us strive to embody this biblical standard, recognizing that our commitment to our wives is a reflection of Christ's love for His church. May we lead our families with grace and integrity, building a marriage rooted in mutual respect, trust, and unwavering love, thus honoring God in all we do.

Men's Leadership Devotional 103

⚒ The Forge Weekly Reflection Sheet

Personal Study & Leadership Accountability Questions

1. **Theme in My Life:** This week's theme was
   "_____"
   In my current life, I see this theme at work in the area of:
   "_____
   _____"

2. **Key Verse Insight:** The Scripture that stood out most to me this week was:
   "_____
   _____"

3. **Because it reminded/taught/convicted me that:**
   "_____
   _____
   _____
   _____"

4. **Connection—The story of _____ made me think about:**
   "_____
   _____"

5. *A similar situation in my life has been:*
   "_____
   _____
   _____"

6. **God's Prompting:** One way I feel God is prompting me to grow or change this week is:
   "_____
   _____
   _____
   _____"

7. **Action Step:** As a man of faith and leadership, one practical step I will take this week is:
   "_____
   _____
   _____
   _____"

8. **Prayer Focus:** I sense the need to bring this to God in prayer:
   "_____
   _____
   _____
   _____"

9. *I also want to lift up these specific people or situations:*
   "_____
   _____
   _____
   _____"

10. **Brotherhood Check-in:**
    One truth I need to share or process with another man is:
    "_____
    _____
    _____
    _____"

11. I plan to connect with: _____ by (day/time): _____

12. Refining at The Forge:
    This week, God is shaping me most in the area of:
    "_____
    _____
    _____
    _____"

13. *I want to remain faithful in this process by:*
    "_____
    _____
    _____
    _____"

Week 13
Fatherhood and Guidance

Providing spiritual and emotional guidance to children, modeling Christ like behavior.

A Father's Influence

Donald was a devoted father of two, balancing work, church commitments, and the daily responsibilities of family life. He wanted to be a good dad, but lately, he felt like he was failing to connect with his teenage son, Noah. Their conversations had become tense, often ending in frustration and misunderstanding. Donald's heart ached as he watched Noah retreat further into himself, spending more time behind a closed bedroom door.

One Saturday afternoon, after another argument about Noah's grades, Donald found himself alone in the garage, feeling defeated. He picked up his Bible, searching for guidance, and landed on Proverbs 22:6: "Train up a child in the way he should go; even when he is old he will not depart from it." He realized that guiding Noah wasn't just about rules and expectations but about showing him the path of faith and love.

Donald then turned to Colossians 3:21: "Fathers, do not provoke your children, lest they become discouraged." He thought about the way he had been handling his frustrations—raising his voice, criticizing, and often letting his impatience take over. Donald saw that his approach was pushing Noah away rather than drawing him closer.

Convicted, Donald knew it was time to change. That evening, he knocked on Noah's door and asked if they could talk. Instead of leading with criticism, Donald sat down and shared his own struggles as a teenager, admitting that he didn't have all the answers. "Noah, I've been hard on you, and I'm sorry. I want to understand what's going on, and I want us to figure this out together. You're important to me, more than any grade or rule."

Noah, surprised by his dad's vulnerability, opened up about the pressures he was facing—fears of failure, the weight of expectations, and the feeling that he could never measure up. Donald listened patiently, fighting the urge to correct or lecture. Instead, he put his arm around Noah and prayed, asking God for wisdom, patience, and a renewed bond between them.

From that day on, Donald made a conscious effort to spend more time with Noah, not just as a disciplinarian but as a guide and friend. They started reading the Bible together, discussing its relevance to Noah's life, and working through challenges with a spirit of collaboration rather than conflict. Donald also made it a point to celebrate Noah's efforts, recognizing his growth rather than just focusing on outcomes.

Donald's approach began to change their relationship. Noah felt supported and encouraged, knowing his father was there to guide him, not just to correct him. The atmosphere in their home shifted from tension to trust, where open conversations replaced arguments, and mutual respect replaced frustration.

Through this journey, Donald learned that fatherhood was more than providing and protecting; it was about modeling Christ-like behavior—showing grace, offering guidance, and nurturing a relationship built on love and understanding. By leading Noah with patience and integrity, Donald was laying the foundation for his son's spiritual and emotional growth, helping him become the man God intended him to be.

Donald's commitment to intentional fatherhood became a powerful witness to his family. He realized that every moment spent guiding his children was an opportunity to reflect Christ's love, planting seeds of faith that would bear fruit for years to come.

> Old Testament: Proverbs 22:6 "Train up a child in the way he should go; even when he is old he will not depart from it."
>
> New Testament: Colossians 3:21 "Fathers, do not provoke your children, lest they become discouraged."

As Christian men, our role as fathers is to provide both spiritual and emotional guidance to our children, modeling Christ-like behavior in all we do. Proverbs 22:6 encourages us to train our children in the way they should go, instilling values and faith that will guide them throughout their lives. In Colossians 3:21, we are reminded to be mindful of our approach, ensuring we do not provoke our children to discouragement, but rather nurture their spirits with love and encouragement. By embodying patience, understanding, and integrity, we set an example that reflects Christ's love and grace. Let us commit to being intentional in our fatherhood, recognizing the profound impact we have on our children's spiritual journeys. May our guidance lead them to a deeper relationship with God, helping them grow into the individuals He has called them to be.

Men's Leadership Devotional

⚒ The Forge Weekly Reflection Sheet

Personal Study & Leadership Accountability Questions

1. **Theme in My Life: This week's theme was**
   "_____"

   In my current life, I see this theme at work in the area of:
   "_____
   _____"

2. **Key Verse Insight: The Scripture that stood out most to me this week was:**
   "_____
   _____"

3. *Because it reminded/taught/convicted me that:*
   "_____
   _____
   _____
   _____"

4. **Connection—The story of _____ made me think about:**
   "_____
   _____"

5. *A similar situation in my life has been:*
   "_____
   _____
   _____
   _____"

6. **God's Prompting:** One way I feel God is prompting me to grow or change this week is:
   "_____
   _____
   _____
   _____"

7. **Action Step:** As a man of faith and leadership, one practical step I will take this week is:
   "_____
   _____
   _____
   _____"

8. **Prayer Focus:** I sense the need to bring this to God in prayer:
   "_____
   _____
   _____
   _____"

9. *I also want to lift up these specific people or situations:*
   "_____
   _____
   _____
   _____"

10. **Brotherhood Check-in:**
    One truth I need to share or process with another man is:
    "_____
    _____
    _____
    _____"

11. I plan to connect with: _____ by (day/time): _____

12. Refining at The Forge:
This week, God is shaping me most in the area of:
"_____
_____
_____
_____"

13. *I want to remain faithful in this process by:*
"_____
_____
_____
_____"

Week 14
Integrity in the Workplace

Upholding ethical standards and integrity in professional settings, reflecting God's values.

Integrity in the Workplace

Ethan was a respected manager at a mid-sized construction company, known for his sharp business acumen and ability to close deals. One afternoon, Ethan's boss called him into the office with an opportunity that could bring in a substantial profit for the company. "We've got a chance to win this big contract," his boss said, sliding a stack of papers across the desk. "But we need to cut a few corners to make our bid more competitive. It's nothing major—just adjusting a few figures to make us look better on paper."

Ethan felt a knot in his stomach. He knew that tweaking the numbers wasn't just a small compromise—it was dishonest. As he sat in his office later, Ethan reflected on Proverbs 16:8: "Better is a little with righteousness than great revenues with injustice." He realized that no amount of profit was worth sacrificing his integrity.

Ethan remembered Colossians 3:23: "Whatever you do, work heartily, as for the Lord and not for men." He had always tried to honor God through his work, striving to be diligent and honest. But now, faced with pressure, Ethan knew this was a test of his commitment to upholding God's values, even when it was difficult.

Ethan prayed for courage and wisdom before heading back to his boss's office. "I've reviewed the contract, and I don't think we should proceed with these changes," he said calmly. "It's not honest, and I believe we can win this bid without compromising our integrity."

His boss frowned, clearly frustrated. "Ethan, everyone does this. It's just how business works. Are you willing to risk losing the contract over this?"

Ethan took a deep breath. "I understand the stakes, but I believe it's better to miss out on a deal than to succeed through dishonest means. We've built our reputation on quality and trust, and I don't want to jeopardize that for short-term gain."

Though the conversation was tense, Ethan's boss reluctantly agreed to submit an honest bid. To their surprise, not only did the company win the contract, but their integrity also earned them respect from the client, who appreciated their straightforward approach.

Ethan's commitment to doing what was right didn't go unnoticed by his colleagues. His actions sparked conversations about ethics and honesty in the workplace, and soon, others began following his example. Ethan's integrity set a new standard, proving that success achieved through righteousness was far more valuable than any financial gain.

Through this experience, Ethan learned that maintaining integrity wasn't always the easiest path, but it was the one that honored God. By working heartily as if serving the Lord, he demonstrated that faithfulness in small decisions builds a foundation of trust and respect that can impact the entire work environment.

Men's Leadership Devotional 117

Ethan's story became a testament to the power of living out one's faith in the workplace. His unwavering commitment to integrity not only brought success but also reflected God's values, influencing those around him and proving that righteousness is the greatest asset a man can carry in his professional life.

> Old Testament: Proverbs 16:8 "Better is a little with righteousness than great revenues with injustice."

> New Testament: Colossians 3:23 "Whatever you do, work heartily, as for the Lord and not for men."

As Christian men, we are called to uphold integrity in the workplace, reflecting God's values in all our professional endeavors. Proverbs 16:8 reminds us that it is better to have little with righteousness than to accumulate wealth through injustice. This truth challenges us to prioritize ethical standards over the allure of profit, ensuring our actions align with God's principles. In Colossians 3:23, we are encouraged to work heartily, as if we are serving the Lord rather than merely fulfilling obligations to men. By committing to integrity, honesty, and diligence in our work, we not only honor God but also set an example for our colleagues and peers. Let us strive to be men of character in our professional lives, knowing that our faithfulness in small things will reflect our commitment to God and can impact others for His glory.

Men's Leadership Devotional 119

⚒ The Forge Weekly Reflection Sheet

Personal Study & Leadership Accountability Questions

1. **Theme in My Life: This week's theme was**
   " _____ "
   In my current life, I see this theme at work in the area of:
   " _____
   _____ "

2. **Key Verse Insight: The Scripture that stood out most to me this week was:**
   " _____
   _____ "

3. *Because it reminded/taught/convicted me that:*
   " _____
   _____
   _____
   _____ "

4. **Connection—The story of _____ made me think about:**
   " _____
   _____ "

5. *A similar situation in my life has been:*
   " _____
   _____
   _____ "

6. **God's Prompting:** One way I feel God is prompting me to grow or change this week is:

   "_____
   _____
   _____
   _____"

7. **Action Step:** As a man of faith and leadership, one practical step I will take this week is:

   "_____
   _____
   _____
   _____"

8. **Prayer Focus:** I sense the need to bring this to God in prayer:

   "_____
   _____
   _____
   _____"

9. *I also want to lift up these specific people or situations:*

   "_____
   _____
   _____
   _____"

10. **Brotherhood Check-in:**
    One truth I need to share or process with another man is:

    "_____
    _____
    _____
    _____"

11. I plan to connect with: _____ by (day/time): _____

12. **Refining at The Forge:**
    This week, God is shaping me most in the area of:
    "_____
    _____
    _____
    _____"

13. *I want to remain faithful in this process by:*
    "_____
    _____
    _____
    _____"

Men's Leadership Devotional 123

Week 15
Community Engagement

Actively participating in and contributing to the community, demonstrating love and service.

Embracing Community Engagement

Ben had always been a man focused on his family, work, and church. While his life was full, he often felt that something was missing—an urge to step beyond his comfort zone and make a difference. One Sunday, during a sermon about community involvement, the pastor quoted Jeremiah 29:7: "But seek the welfare of the city where I have sent you into exile, and pray to the Lord on its behalf…" Ben felt a nudge in his heart, realizing he had been content to live in his community without truly engaging with it.

That week, Ben noticed a flyer about a local park cleanup initiative. His neighborhood had struggled with neglect, and the park had become a place few families wanted to visit. Remembering Galatians 6:10—"So then, as we have opportunity, let us do good to everyone…"—Ben decided to join the effort. Early Saturday morning, he showed up at the park, gloves on and ready to work.

As Ben picked up trash and pulled weeds, he met neighbors he had never spoken to before. There was Maria, a single mom who brought her young son, hoping to make the park safer for him. And Mr. Thompson, a retired teacher, shared stories of when the park was a hub of community activity. They worked together, chatting and laughing, finding joy in the simple act of caring for their shared space.

Inspired by the day, Ben began to see his community with new eyes. He noticed the needs around him—the elderly neighbor struggling with yard work, the food pantry in need of volunteers, and the youth center looking for mentors. Ben started organizing small service projects, inviting friends and family to join him. They painted over graffiti, delivered meals, and spent time with kids who needed positive role models.

Through these efforts, Ben's neighborhood began to change. People who rarely spoke to each other started to connect, sharing not just tasks but their lives. The park, once neglected, became a gathering place for families again, filled with the sound of children's laughter and neighbors greeting each other warmly.

One evening, after a community cookout, Ben's wife, Sarah, smiled at him and said, "You've really made a difference here." Ben shook his head, feeling humbled. "It's not just me—it's all of us. We're doing what God called us to do, loving our neighbors and seeking the welfare of our city."

Ben realized that engaging with his community was more than just volunteering—it was an expression of his faith. By stepping into the needs around him, he was living out the principles of Jeremiah 29:7 and Galatians 6:10, demonstrating God's love through service. His actions created ripples of kindness, fostering a spirit of unity and hope in a place that had felt forgotten.

Through his commitment to community engagement, Ben discovered the joy of serving others. He learned that every small act of kindness was an opportunity to reflect

Christ's compassion and make a lasting impact. His life became a testament to the power of stepping out in faith, showing that when we seek the welfare of our communities, we bring God's kingdom a little closer to home.

> Old Testament: Jeremiah 29:7 "But seek the welfare of the city where I have sent you into exile, and pray to the Lord on its behalf..."
>
> New Testament: Galatians 6:10 "So then, as we have opportunity, let us do good to everyone..."

As Christian men, we are called to actively engage with and contribute to our communities, demonstrating love and service in tangible ways. Jeremiah 29:7 encourages us to seek the welfare of the city where we find ourselves, reminding us that our prayers and actions can bring about positive change even in challenging circumstances. In Galatians 6:10, we are urged to do good to everyone as opportunities arise, highlighting the importance of our intentionality in serving others. By stepping into the needs of our communities, we not only fulfill our call as followers of Christ but also reflect His love and compassion to those around us. Let us commit to being active participants in our neighborhoods, using our gifts and resources to uplift others and foster a spirit of unity and hope, knowing that through our service, we can make a lasting impact for God's kingdom.

🛠 The Forge Weekly Reflection Sheet

Personal Study & Leadership Accountability Questions

1. **Theme in My Life:** This week's theme was
   " _____ "
   In my current life, I see this theme at work in the area of:
   " _____
   _____ "

2. **Key Verse Insight:** The Scripture that stood out most to me this week was:
   " _____
   _____ "

3. *Because it reminded/taught/convicted me that:*
   " _____
   _____
   _____
   _____ "

4. **Connection**—The story of _____ made me think about:
   " _____
   _____ "

5. *A similar situation in my life has been:*
   " _____
   _____
   _____
   _____ "

6. **God's Prompting:** One way I feel God is prompting me to grow or change this week is:
   "_____
   _____
   _____
   _____"

7. **Action Step:** As a man of faith and leadership, one practical step I will take this week is:
   "_____
   _____
   _____
   _____"

8. **Prayer Focus:** I sense the need to bring this to God in prayer:
   "_____
   _____
   _____
   _____"

9. *I also want to lift up these specific people or situations:*
   "_____
   _____
   _____
   _____"

10. **Brotherhood Check-in:**
    One truth I need to share or process with another man is:
    "_____
    _____
    _____
    _____"

11. I plan to connect with: _____ by (day/time): _____

12. Refining at The Forge:
This week, God is shaping me most in the area of:
"_____
_____
_____
_____"

13. I want to remain faithful in this process by:
"_____
_____
_____
_____"

SECTION 3

Men on Mission: Courage, Conviction, and Calling

(Weeks 16–20)

A man on mission doesn't drift—he advances. In this stretch, you'll wrestle with your call to live boldly and lead faithfully. These aren't just abstract ideas. They're anchored in witness, accountability, moral conviction, and the grit to keep going when the cost is high.

This section will press into your spiritual backbone. Where are you standing firm? Where are you shrinking back? The goal isn't perfection—it's obedience. You'll explore how courage, humility, and servant-hearted strength set you apart in a culture that's forgotten what godly masculinity even looks like. It's time to reclaim it.

Week 16
Witnessing and Evangelism

Sharing the gospel and living as a witness to Christ in everyday life.

A Quiet Witness

Alex was an ordinary man with a busy life—work, family, and church commitments kept him on the go. While he loved God deeply, the idea of witnessing and evangelism often felt intimidating. He wasn't a preacher, and he didn't feel like he had the right words to share the gospel. But Alex knew that God was calling him to be more intentional in living out his faith, especially after reading Isaiah 49:6: "I will make you as a light for the nations..." He realized that his life could shine God's light, even in simple, everyday moments.

One day at work, Alex noticed his coworker, Brian, sitting alone during lunch, looking troubled. Brian had recently gone through a messy divorce and was struggling to keep his spirits up. Alex hesitated, unsure of what to say, but he felt a nudge in his heart to reach out. Remembering Matthew 28:19—"Go therefore and make disciples of all nations"—Alex knew he couldn't ignore this opportunity to be a witness.

Alex sat down next to Brian and asked how he was doing. Brian opened up, sharing his pain and feelings of hopelessness. Instead of offering platitudes, Alex listened, genuinely caring about what Brian was going through. "I'm sorry you're going through this," Alex said softly. "I've been through some tough times too, and I've found that my faith in God really helps. If you ever want to talk about it, I'm here for you."

Brian looked surprised. He knew Alex was a Christian, but this was the first time Alex had ever spoken so openly about his faith. Over the next few weeks, Alex continued to check in on Brian, offering encouragement, prayer, and support. He didn't push or preach; he simply shared his own experiences, pointing Brian to the hope he had found in Christ.

One afternoon, as they were leaving work, Brian said, "You know, Alex, I've been thinking about what you said about faith. I've never really considered it before, but seeing how you handle life makes me curious. How do you keep your peace?"

Alex smiled, grateful for the chance to share. "It's Jesus," he said simply. "He's changed my life, and I know He can change yours too." Alex invited Brian to church, and to his surprise, Brian accepted. That Sunday, Brian heard the gospel message, and for the first time, it resonated deeply with him.

As Brian began his own journey of faith, Alex realized that witnessing wasn't about having all the right answers or a perfect script—it was about living authentically, showing Christ's love, and being willing to share the hope within. Alex's quiet witness had a profound impact, opening the door for Brian to experience God's grace.

Through this experience, Alex learned that evangelism didn't have to be complicated. By being present, compassionate, and bold enough to speak about his faith, he became a light in Brian's dark moment. Alex's willingness to step out of his comfort zone showed him that God could use ordinary conversations to change lives.

Alex's life became a living testament to Isaiah 49:6 and Matthew 28:19, reflecting God's call to be a light and make disciples. He understood that every day was an opportunity to witness, not just with words, but through actions that pointed others to Christ. His faithfulness in small moments contributed to the fulfillment of the Great Commission, reminding him that God's power works through simple, obedient steps.

> Old Testament: Isaiah 49:6 "It is too light a thing that you should be my servant to raise up the tribes of Jacob and to bring back the preserved of Israel; I will make you as a light for the nations..."
>
> New Testament: Matthew 28:19 "Go therefore and make disciples of all nations..."

As Christian men, we are called to be bold witnesses for Christ, sharing the gospel and living out our faith in every aspect of our lives. Isaiah 49:6 reminds us that we are called not only to serve within our own circles but to be a light for the nations, reflecting God's love and truth to a world in need. In Matthew 28:19, Jesus commissions us to go and make disciples of all nations, emphasizing that our mission extends beyond our immediate surroundings. This call invites us to engage with others, demonstrating Christ's love through our actions and words, and to share the hope we have in Him. Let us commit to being intentional in our witnessing, recognizing that our everyday lives can serve as powerful testimonies of God's grace and transformative power. May we seize every opportunity to point others to Christ, knowing that through our faithfulness, we can contribute to the fulfillment of the Great Commission and impact lives for eternity.

⚒ The Forge Weekly Reflection Sheet

Personal Study & Leadership Accountability Questions

1. **Theme in My Life: This week's theme was**
   "_____"
   In my current life, I see this theme at work in the area of:
   "_____
   _____"

2. **Key Verse Insight: The Scripture that stood out most to me this week was:**
   "_____
   _____"

3. *Because it reminded/taught/convicted me that:*
   "_____
   _____
   _____"

4. **Connection—The story of _____ made me think about:**
   "_____
   _____"

5. *A similar situation in my life has been:*
   "_____
   _____
   _____"

6. **God's Prompting: One way I feel God is prompting me to grow or change this week is:**
   "_____
   _____
   _____
   _____"

7. **Action Step: As a man of faith and leadership, one practical step I will take this week is:**
   "_____
   _____
   _____
   _____"

8. **Prayer Focus: I sense the need to bring this to God in prayer:**
   "_____
   _____
   _____
   _____"

9. *I also want to lift up these specific people or situations:*
   "_____
   _____
   _____
   _____"

10. **Brotherhood Check-in:**
    One truth I need to share or process with another man is:
    "_____
    _____
    _____
    _____"

11. I plan to connect with: _____ by (day/time): _____

12. **Refining at The Forge:**
    This week, God is shaping me most in the area of:
    "_____
    _____
    _____
    _____ "

13. *I want to remain faithful in this process by:*
    "_____
    _____
    _____
    _____ "

Week 17
Accountability and Transparency

Engaging in mutual accountability with other men, fostering growth and responsibility.

Strength in Accountability

Matt had always prided himself on being independent, handling his struggles quietly and keeping his challenges to himself. He was active in his church and known as a reliable guy, but beneath the surface, Matt was battling a persistent issue: he was caught in a cycle of anger and frustration that often spilled over at home. Arguments with his wife were becoming frequent, and he found himself losing patience with his kids more often than he wanted to admit.

One Sunday after church, Matt's friend, John, pulled him aside. "Hey, Matt, you've seemed a little off lately. Everything okay?" Kylehad been in a men's group with Matt for years, and he knew when something wasn't right. Matt hesitated, tempted to brush it off with the usual, "I'm fine." But Proverbs 27:17 came to his mind: "Iron sharpens iron, and one man sharpens another." Matt realized that hiding his struggles wasn't helping anyone, least of all himself.

"Actually, John, I've been having a hard time," Matt confessed. He opened up about his anger, his fights at home, and the shame he felt over losing control.

Kyle listened without judgment, nodding with understanding. He then shared his own past struggles and how accountability had helped him find healing. Kyle gently reminded Matt of Galatians 6:1: "Brothers, if anyone is caught in any transgression, you who are spiritual should restore him in a spirit of gentleness…"

"Matt, you don't have to handle this alone. Let's meet up regularly and keep each other accountable," Kyle suggested. "We can pray, talk through things, and support one another. It's okay to admit we don't have it all together."

Matt agreed, and the two men began meeting weekly over coffee. Their conversations were honest, filled with moments of vulnerability and encouragement. Kyle held Matt accountable, asking him the tough questions about his reactions and helping him develop strategies to manage his anger. They didn't just focus on Matt's struggles but celebrated each victory, no matter how small.

Over time, Matt noticed a change. The moments of anger still came, but now he was equipped with the tools to pause, pray, and respond differently. He began to restore the peace in his home, slowly rebuilding trust with his wife and creating a calmer environment for his kids. The accountability he had feared at first became a source of strength, pushing him closer to God and refining his character.

One morning, as Matt reflected on his journey, he realized that John's willingness to reach out had been a turning point. Their accountability partnership had sharpened them both, helping them grow as husbands, fathers, and men of faith. Matt saw the value of Proverbs 27:17 lived out in their friendship: iron truly did sharpen iron.

Through their commitment to mutual accountability, Matt and Kylecultivated a space where they could be transparent, challenge each other, and walk together through the highs and lows of life. Matt learned that accountability wasn't about shame—it was about support, growth, and becoming the men God called them to be.

Matt's experience underscored the power of community and the importance of being open to correction and encouragement. By engaging in accountability, Matt found healing and helped foster a culture of transparency and growth among his brothers in Christ. He understood that when men come together in honesty and grace, they not only sharpen each other but also reflect God's transformative love to the world.

> Old Testament: Proverbs 27:17 "Iron sharpens iron, and one man sharpens another."
>
> New Testament: Galatians 6:1 "Brothers, if anyone is caught in any transgression, you who are spiritual should restore him in a spirit of gentleness..."

As Christian men, engaging in mutual accountability with one another is essential for our growth and responsibility in faith. Proverbs 27:17 reminds us that "iron sharpens iron," highlighting the strength and refinement that comes from relationships rooted in honesty and encouragement. In Galatians 6:1, we are called to restore one another gently when we stumble, emphasizing the importance of support and grace within our community. By opening ourselves to accountability, we not only strengthen our own walk with Christ but also create a culture of transparency and growth among our brothers. Let us commit to fostering deep connections, where we can share our struggles and victories, challenge each other to live righteously, and celebrate God's work in our lives.

144 The Forge

Together, we can sharpen one another, becoming the men God has called us to be, and reflecting His love and truth to the world around us.

Men's Leadership Devotional 145

✖ The Forge Weekly Reflection Sheet

Personal Study & Leadership Accountability Questions

1. **Theme in My Life:** This week's theme was
   "_____"
   In my current life, I see this theme at work in the area of:
   "_____
   _____"

2. **Key Verse Insight:** The Scripture that stood out most to me this week was:
   "_____
   _____"

3. *Because it reminded/taught/convicted me that:*
   "_____
   _____
   _____
   _____"

4. **Connection—The story of _____ made me think about:**
   "_____
   _____"

5. *A similar situation in my life has been:*
   "_____
   _____
   _____"

6. **God's Prompting:** One way I feel God is prompting me to grow or change this week is:

   " _____
   _____
   _____
   _____ "

7. **Action Step:** As a man of faith and leadership, one practical step I will take this week is:

   " _____
   _____
   _____
   _____ "

8. **Prayer Focus:** I sense the need to bring this to God in prayer:

   " _____
   _____
   _____
   _____ "

9. *I also want to lift up these specific people or situations:*

   " _____
   _____
   _____
   _____ "

10. **Brotherhood Check-in:**
    One truth I need to share or process with another man is:

    " _____
    _____
    _____
    _____ "

11. I plan to connect with: _____ by (day/time): _____

12. **Refining at The Forge:**
    This week, God is shaping me most in the area of:
    "_____
    _____
    _____
    _____"

13. *I want to remain faithful in this process by:*
    "_____
    _____
    _____
    _____"

Week 18
Patience and Understanding

Practicing patience in leadership, showing grace to others in challenging situations.

Leading with Patience and Grace

Mike was the foreman of a construction crew known for tight deadlines and high-pressure projects. He took pride in getting the job done, but recently, things had been chaotic. The weather had delayed their timeline, and the team was feeling the strain. One afternoon, as Mike inspected the site, he found that a critical mistake had been made—the measurements were off, and a whole section of the foundation would need to be redone. Frustration surged within him; this error would cost them valuable time and money.

Mike marched over to his crew, ready to let them have it, but he paused, recalling Proverbs 14:29: "Whoever is slow to anger has great understanding, but he who has a hasty temper exalts folly." He knew that losing his temper wouldn't fix the mistake; it would only escalate the stress and discourage his team. He took a deep breath, letting the wisdom of James 1:19 guide him: "Let every person be quick to hear, slow to speak, slow to anger."

Instead of shouting, Mike called the crew together calmly. "Let's figure out what went wrong and how we can fix it," he said, his voice steady. Mike listened as his team explained the mix-up—there had been a miscommunication about the blueprint. One of the newer workers, Jason, nervously admitted his role in the error, clearly expecting a harsh response. But instead of lashing out, Mike nodded, understanding that mistakes were part of learning.

"Thanks for owning up, Jason," Mike said, placing a hand on his shoulder. "We've all been there. Let's work together to get this right." The crew was relieved; they expected anger but found grace.

Mike worked alongside them, showing how to correct the issue and making sure everyone was clear on the steps going forward. The atmosphere shifted from tension to teamwork, and the mistake became a learning opportunity rather than a setback. Mike's patience not only preserved morale but also strengthened the crew's trust in his leadership.

Later that day, as they wrapped up, Jason approached Mike. "I thought you'd be furious," he admitted. "But the way you handled it—thanks for giving me a chance to fix my mistake."

Mike smiled, grateful for the reminder of the impact patience could have. "We're all learning, Jason. It's not just about getting the job done but doing it with understanding and respect. We're in this together."

Through this experience, Mike learned that true leadership wasn't just about directing a team but about guiding with patience and grace, especially when things went wrong. His calm response fostered an environment where his crew felt supported rather than condemned, and they became more committed to their work and to each other.

Mike's practice of patience and understanding became a hallmark of his leadership, reflecting Christ's love in every interaction. He realized that by being slow to anger and quick to listen, he was not only leading well but also creating a culture where mistakes could be met with grace and opportunities for growth.

This approach helped Mike build a foundation of trust and respect within his team, making them stronger and more unified. By embodying patience in challenging situations, Mike showed that leadership rooted in understanding was not a sign of weakness but a reflection of Christ's strength. His actions served as a reminder that every moment of grace extended was an opportunity to honor God and lead others with a heart aligned with His will.

> Old Testament: Proverbs 14:29 "Whoever is slow to anger has great understanding, but he who has a hasty temper exalts folly."
>
> New Testament: James 1:19 "Know this, my beloved brothers: let every person be quick to hear, slow to speak, slow to anger."

As Christian men, practicing patience and understanding in our leadership is vital, especially when faced with challenging situations. Proverbs 14:29 teaches us that a slow temper reflects great understanding, while a hasty response leads to folly. In James 1:19, we are encouraged to be quick to hear, slow to speak, and slow to anger, reminding us of the importance of listening and responding thoughtfully. By embodying patience, we create an environment where grace can thrive, allowing us to lead with compassion and wisdom. Let us commit to cultivating a spirit of understanding, recognizing that every interaction is an opportunity to reflect Christ's love. As we practice patience in our leadership, we not only foster growth in ourselves and others but also create a foundation of trust and respect that honors God in all we

152 The Forge

do. May our responses be filled with grace, allowing us to navigate challenges with a heart aligned with His will.

⚒ The Forge Weekly Reflection Sheet

Personal Study & Leadership Accountability Questions

1. **Theme in My Life: This week's theme was**
   "_____"

   In my current life, I see this theme at work in the area of:
   "_____
   _____"

2. **Key Verse Insight: The Scripture that stood out most to me this week was:**
   "_____
   _____"

3. *Because it reminded/taught/convicted me that:*
   "_____
   _____
   _____
   _____"

4. **Connection—The story of _____ made me think about:**
   "_____
   _____"

5. *A similar situation in my life has been:*
   "_____
   _____
   _____
   _____"

6. **God's Prompting:** One way I feel God is prompting me to grow or change this week is:
   "_____
   _____
   _____
   _____"

7. **Action Step:** As a man of faith and leadership, one practical step I will take this week is:
   "_____
   _____
   _____
   _____"

8. **Prayer Focus:** I sense the need to bring this to God in prayer:
   "_____
   _____
   _____
   _____"

9. *I also want to lift up these specific people or situations:*
   "_____
   _____
   _____
   _____"

10. **Brotherhood Check-in:**
    One truth I need to share or process with another man is:
    "_____
    _____
    _____
    _____"

Men's Leadership Devotional

11. I plan to connect with: _____ by (day/time): _____

12. **Refining at The Forge:**
    This week, God is shaping me most in the area of:
    "_____
    _____
    _____
    _____"

13. *I want to remain faithful in this process by:*
    "_____
    _____
    _____
    _____"

Week 19
Cultivating a Servant Heart

Leading by example through acts of service, placing others' needs before personal desires.

Leading with a Servant's Heart

Chris was a respected leader in his church, always willing to lend a hand and organize events. Yet, deep down, he knew that while he was busy doing the work, his heart wasn't always in the right place. He often found himself driven by recognition rather than a true desire to serve. One Sunday, while preparing for a church outreach event, Chris overheard an elderly couple struggling to clean up a small spill in the fellowship hall. They were part of the team, but their efforts were often overlooked.

Chris felt a tug in his spirit, recalling Micah 6:8: "He has told you, O man, what is good; and what does the Lord require of you but to do justice, and to love kindness, and to walk humbly with your God?" Chris realized that service was more than tasks; it was about seeing and loving people in the everyday, small moments. The words of John 13:14 also resonated deeply: "If I then, your Lord and Teacher, have washed your feet, you also ought to wash one another's feet." Jesus had modeled the ultimate act of humble service, setting a standard that Chris knew he was called to follow.

Putting down his clipboard, Chris walked over to the couple and quietly began helping them clean the spill.

"Thank you for all you do here," Chris said sincerely. They smiled, surprised by his kindness. It was a simple act, but it shifted something in Chris's heart. He realized that true leadership wasn't about being in charge—it was about serving without the need for recognition.

Later that week, Chris felt inspired to put his new perspective into action. He organized a "Service Saturday" for the church, but instead of leading from the front as usual, Chris decided to take a different role. He signed up for the least glamorous task—cleaning the bathrooms—choosing to serve quietly and without fanfare.

As Chris scrubbed floors and cleaned toilets, he reflected on Jesus washing His disciples' feet. He felt a deep sense of joy and humility, understanding that this simple work was a way to love his community and honor God. It wasn't about being seen; it was about being faithful.

When the day was over, several church members approached Chris, noticing his change in approach. "You really set an example today," one of the volunteers said. "It's inspiring to see you serve like that."

Chris smiled, grateful for the lesson God was teaching him. "I just wanted to follow Jesus' example," he said. "Serving is a privilege, not a chore."

Through his actions, Chris learned that cultivating a servant heart was more powerful than any position or title. By prioritizing the needs of others and embracing humility, he found a deeper connection to God's calling on his life. His willingness to serve quietly and wholeheartedly inspired others, creating a ripple effect of kindness and selflessness throughout the church.

Chris's leadership took on new meaning as he continued to look for ways to serve behind the scenes, placing others before himself. His actions reflected the heart of Christ, showing that true greatness lies not in being served, but in serving.

By leading through acts of service, Chris demonstrated that a servant's heart transforms not only the leader but also the community around him. His commitment to doing justice, loving kindness, and walking humbly with God became a living testament to the power of servant leadership, echoing Christ's call to love one another in the most practical and personal ways.

> Old Testament: Micah 6:8 "He has told you, O man, what is good; and what does the Lord require of you but to do justice, and to love kindness, and to walk humbly with your God?"
>
> New Testament: John 13:14 "If I then, your Lord and Teacher, have washed your feet, you also ought to wash one another's feet."

As Christian men, cultivating a servant heart is essential to our leadership, exemplifying Christ's love through acts of service and humility. Micah 6:8 reminds us of God's call to do justice, love kindness, and walk humbly with Him, urging us to prioritize the needs of others over our own desires. In John 13:14, Jesus, our Lord and Teacher, demonstrates true leadership by washing the feet of His disciples, setting a powerful example of service. Let us commit to leading by example, actively seeking ways to serve those around us—whether in our families, workplaces, or communities. By placing others first and embracing humility, we reflect Christ's character and fulfill His command to love one another. May our servant hearts not only transform our own lives but also inspire those around us to seek the same selfless love, building a community grounded in kindness and grace.

🛠 The Forge Weekly Reflection Sheet

Personal Study & Leadership Accountability Questions

1. **Theme in My Life: This week's theme was**
   " _____ "
   In my current life, I see this theme at work in the area of:
   " _____
   _____ "

2. **Key Verse Insight: The Scripture that stood out most to me this week was:**
   " _____
   _____ "

3. ***Because it reminded/taught/convicted me that:***
   " _____
   _____
   _____
   _____ "

4. **Connection—The story of _____ made me think about:**
   " _____
   _____ "

5. ***A similar situation in my life has been:***
   " _____
   _____
   _____
   _____ "

6. **God's Prompting:** One way I feel God is prompting me to grow or change this week is:

   "_____
   _____
   _____
   _____"

7. **Action Step:** As a man of faith and leadership, one practical step I will take this week is:

   "_____
   _____
   _____
   _____"

8. **Prayer Focus:** I sense the need to bring this to God in prayer:

   "_____
   _____
   _____
   _____"

9. *I also want to lift up these specific people or situations:*

   "_____
   _____
   _____
   _____"

10. **Brotherhood Check-in:**
    One truth I need to share or process with another man is:

    "_____
    _____
    _____
    _____"

11. I plan to connect with: _____ by (day/time): _____

12. Refining at The Forge:
   This week, God is shaping me most in the area of:
   "_____
   _____
   _____
   _____ "

13. *I want to remain faithful in this process by:*
   "_____
   _____
   _____
   _____ "

Week 20
Moral and Ethical Leadership

Upholding high moral standards and promoting justice in all aspects of life.

Standing Firm in Moral Leadership

Jason was a respected manager at a local manufacturing company, known for his work ethic and commitment to fairness. The company was experiencing rapid growth, and with new opportunities came increased pressure to meet targets and cut costs. One afternoon, during a leadership meeting, the CEO presented a proposal to save significant expenses by outsourcing a portion of their work to a less regulated overseas supplier. While the move promised financial gains, Jason knew that the supplier had questionable labor practices, including unsafe working conditions and low wages.

As the room buzzed with excitement over the potential savings, Jason felt a knot in his stomach. He thought of Proverbs 29:2: "When the righteous increase, the people rejoice, but when the wicked rule, the people groan." Jason knew that their decision could impact lives far beyond their office walls. He looked around the table and realized that if no one stood up for what was right, the company would be complicit in exploiting vulnerable workers.

When the CEO asked for feedback, Jason spoke up, his voice steady but firm. "I understand the financial benefits, but I can't support this decision. Partnering with a supplier that exploits its workers goes against everything we stand for. We need to be a company that values people over profits."

The room fell silent. Some colleagues shifted uncomfortably, while others nodded in quiet agreement. The CEO frowned, clearly displeased. "Jason, this is business. Sometimes you have to make tough choices."

Jason took a deep breath, recalling Titus 2:7: "Show yourself in all respects to be a model of good works, and in your teaching show integrity, dignity…" He knew that this was his moment to uphold moral leadership, no matter the cost. "I believe we can be profitable without compromising our values. If we want our employees, customers, and community to trust us, we need to lead with integrity."

The CEO paused, then sighed. "We'll revisit this," he said reluctantly, moving on to the next agenda item. But Jason's words had planted a seed. Over the next few days, several colleagues approached him, expressing their gratitude for his courage and voicing their own concerns. Together, they presented alternative options to the CEO that prioritized ethical suppliers, showing that doing the right thing didn't have to come at the expense of business success.

Eventually, the company chose to partner with a supplier that met their ethical standards, preserving their reputation and aligning their practices with their values. The decision not only benefited their business but also sent a powerful message about the importance of moral leadership.

Through this experience, Jason learned that standing up for what is right often means standing alone—but it's a stand worth taking. His commitment to high moral standards and justice set a new tone within the company, encouraging others to speak up and act with integrity. The ripple effect of his decision was felt far beyond the boardroom, fostering a culture where ethical leadership became the norm, not the exception.

Jason's actions demonstrated that true leadership isn't just about achieving goals but about how those goals are reached. By embodying the principles of Proverbs 29:2 and Titus 2:7, Jason created a legacy of moral leadership that honored God and inspired others to pursue righteousness. He proved that when the righteous lead, everyone benefits, and that a commitment to integrity can light the way in even the most challenging situations.

> Old Testament: Proverbs 29:2 "When the righteous increase, the people rejoice, but when the wicked rule, the people groan."
>
> New Testament: Titus 2:7 "Show yourself in all respects to be a model of good works, and in your teaching show integrity, dignity..."

As Christian men, we are called to uphold high moral standards and promote justice in every aspect of our lives, embodying the values of our faith. Proverbs 29:2 reminds us that when the righteous lead, the people rejoice, highlighting the profound impact of moral leadership on the community. In Titus 2:7, we are encouraged to be models of good works, demonstrating integrity and dignity in our actions and teachings. By committing to ethical leadership, we not only reflect Christ's character but also inspire those around us to pursue righteousness. Let us strive to be men of principle, standing firm against injustice and advocating for what is right. As we lead with integrity, we create a legacy that honors God and fosters an environment where all can thrive in His love and truth. May our commitment to moral leadership shine as a

168 The Forge

beacon of hope and encouragement in a world that desperately needs it.

Men's Leadership Devotional 169

✴ The Forge Weekly Reflection Sheet

Personal Study & Leadership Accountability Questions

1. **Theme in My Life: This week's theme was**
   "_____"

   In my current life, I see this theme at work in the area of:
   "_____
   _____"

2. **Key Verse Insight: The Scripture that stood out most to me this week was:**
   "_____
   _____"

3. *Because it reminded/taught/convicted me that:*
   "_____
   _____
   _____
   _____"

4. **Connection—The story of _____ made me think about:**
   "_____
   _____"

5. *A similar situation in my life has been:*
   "_____
   _____
   _____
   _____"

6. **God's Prompting: One way I feel God is prompting me to grow or change this week is:**
   "_____
   _____
   _____
   _____"

7. **Action Step: As a man of faith and leadership, one practical step I will take this week is:**
   "_____
   _____
   _____
   _____"

8. **Prayer Focus: I sense the need to bring this to God in prayer:**
   "_____
   _____
   _____
   _____"

9. *I also want to lift up these specific people or situations:*
   "_____
   _____
   _____
   _____"

10. **Brotherhood Check-in:**
    One truth I need to share or process with another man is:
    "_____
    _____
    _____
    _____"

11. I plan to connect with: _____ by (day/time): _____

12. **Refining at The Forge:**
    This week, God is shaping me most in the area of:
    "_____
    _____
    _____
    _____"

13. *I want to remain faithful in this process by:*
    "_____
    _____
    _____
    _____"

SECTION 4

Living as Leaders: Impacting Family and Culture

(Weeks 21–30)

Leadership isn't just something you do at work or church—it's how you shape the culture of your home, how you respond to temptation, how you treat your neighbors, and how you carry yourself when no one is clapping. This section gets deeply personal. It walks into your living room, your thought life, your marriage bed, and your neighborhood block.

You'll be challenged to lead through service, create a culture of honor, engage a broken world with compassion, and model resilience when things get hard. It's about showing up, staying faithful, and making your leadership felt in the places that matter most.

Week 21
Raising Godly Children

Intentional parenting that instills faith and values in children, preparing them for life.

The Gift of Intentional Parenting

Steven loved being a father. He cherished his two young sons, Ethan and Caleb, and knew that they were a blessing from the Lord. Yet, like many busy fathers, Steven often found himself caught up in the daily grind—work, errands, and the endless cycle of responsibilities. He wanted his boys to grow up strong in their faith, but he often wondered if he was doing enough to guide them spiritually.

One evening, after a long day at work, Steven sat on the porch with his Bible, feeling overwhelmed. As he read Psalm 127:3—"Behold, children are a heritage from the Lord, the fruit of the womb a reward"—he realized that his boys were not just his responsibility but his greatest gift. The verse stirred something in him; he knew he needed to be more intentional in his parenting, not just providing for his sons but truly investing in their hearts and faith.

Steven thought of 2 Timothy 1:5, which spoke of the sincere faith passed down through generations: "I am reminded of your sincere faith, a faith that dwelt first in your grandmother Lois and your mother Eunice…" Steven knew that the faith of the next generation depended on what was modeled and taught today. He felt convicted to be a father who actively instilled God's values in his children, just as Timothy's mother and grandmother had done.

The next morning, Steven gathered Ethan and Caleb around the breakfast table. "We're going to start doing something new," he said, smiling. "Every day, we're going to read a Bible story together and talk about what it means." The boys were excited, especially when Steven pulled out a colorful children's Bible filled with stories and illustrations.

As they began their daily devotions, Steven encouraged the boys to ask questions and share their thoughts. They talked about David's courage, Daniel's faithfulness, and Jesus' love for everyone. Steven made sure to relate the lessons to their everyday lives, teaching them that God was not just a character in a book but a real and loving presence in their world.

Steven also made time for intentional moments of prayer, asking each son to share their worries and thank God for their blessings. He taught them simple, heartfelt prayers, showing them that talking to God was as natural as talking to their dad.

Over time, Steven noticed a beautiful change in his home. The boys began to pray on their own, thanking God before meals and asking for His help with school and friendships. Ethan even reminded Steven to pray before a big meeting at work, showing that the lessons were taking root in their young hearts.

One night, as Steven tucked Caleb into bed, his son hugged him tightly and said, "Dad, I love that we learn about God together." Steven's heart swelled with gratitude. He realized that these small, everyday moments were shaping his sons' faith in profound ways.

Through his commitment to intentional parenting, Steven saw firsthand the impact of living out Psalm 127:3 and 2 Timothy 1:5. He understood that raising godly children wasn't about perfection but about presence—showing up every day to teach, guide, and love with a heart turned toward God.

Steven's efforts were building a legacy of faith that would carry his sons through life's challenges, preparing them to stand strong in their own relationship with God. He knew that the seeds he was planting now would bear fruit for generations, just as Lois and Eunice's faith had impacted Timothy.

Steven's story became a testament to the power of intentional parenting. By prioritizing time with his children, teaching them God's Word, and modeling sincere faith, he was equipping Ethan and Caleb with the values and beliefs they needed to navigate the world. Through his love and guidance, Steven was fulfilling his God-given role, raising his boys to shine brightly for Christ and carry forward the legacy of faith he had worked so diligently to impart.

> Old Testament: Psalm 127:3 "Behold, children are a heritage from the Lord, the fruit of the womb a reward."
>
> New Testament: 2 Timothy 1:5 "I am reminded of your sincere faith, a faith that dwelt first in your grandmother Lois and your mother Eunice..."

As Christian men, we are entrusted with the sacred responsibility of raising godly children, intentionally instilling faith and values that prepare them for life's challenges. Psalm 127:3 reminds us that children are a heritage from the Lord, a precious gift that comes with the privilege of nurturing their spiritual growth. In 2 Timothy

1:5, we see the impact of a sincere faith passed down through generations, highlighting the importance of our role in modeling and teaching the faith. Let us be deliberate in our parenting, creating an environment where faith flourishes and values are deeply rooted. By investing time in prayer, teaching, and open conversations, we can guide our children to develop their own relationship with God. May our efforts lead them to a strong foundation of faith, preparing them to shine brightly in the world and carry forward the legacy of love and belief we have imparted to them.

Men's Leadership Devotional 179

✖ The Forge Weekly Reflection Sheet

Personal Study & Leadership Accountability Questions

1. **Theme in My Life: This week's theme was**
   "_____"

   In my current life, I see this theme at work in the area of:
   "_____
   _____"

2. **Key Verse Insight: The Scripture that stood out most to me this week was:**
   "_____
   _____"

3. *Because it reminded/taught/convicted me that:*
   "_____
   _____
   _____
   _____"

4. **Connection—The story of _____ made me think about:**
   "_____
   _____"

5. *A similar situation in my life has been:*
   "_____
   _____
   _____
   _____"

6. **God's Prompting: One way I feel God is prompting me to grow or change this week is:**
   "_____
   _____
   _____
   _____"

7. **Action Step: As a man of faith and leadership, one practical step I will take this week is:**
   "_____
   _____
   _____
   _____"

8. **Prayer Focus: I sense the need to bring this to God in prayer:**
   "_____
   _____
   _____
   _____"

9. *I also want to lift up these specific people or situations:*
   "_____
   _____
   _____
   _____"

10. **Brotherhood Check-in:**
    One truth I need to share or process with another man is:
    "_____
    _____
    _____
    _____"

11. I plan to connect with: _____ by (day/time): _____

12. Refining at The Forge:
    This week, God is shaping me most in the area of:
    "_____
    _____
    _____
    _____"

13. *I want to remain faithful in this process by:*
    "_____
    _____
    _____
    _____"

Week 22
Balancing Work and Family

Striving for balance between professional responsibilities and family commitments.

Balancing the Scales of Leadership

Andrew, a dedicated father and successful business executive, found himself trapped in a cycle of endless meetings, late nights, and constant emails. The demands of his job were relentless, and though he loved his family deeply, he often felt torn between his professional responsibilities and his desire to be present at home. One Saturday afternoon, as he prepared to tackle yet another work project, his young daughter approached him with a hopeful smile and an invitation to play outside.

Caught between the pressure of deadlines and the pull of his daughter's innocent request, Andrew remembered the words from Exodus 20:8: "Remember the Sabbath day, to keep it holy." He realized that his constant drive to achieve was eroding the sacred time meant for rest, reflection, and family. Jesus' words in Mark 6:31 echoed in his heart: "Come away by yourselves to a desolate place and rest a while."

Inspired by these scriptures, Andrew made a decision: he turned off his computer, put away his phone, and stepped outside to join his daughter. As they laughed and played together, Andrew felt a sense of peace that he hadn't experienced in a long time. That simple act of setting aside his work to reconnect with his family became a turning point. Andrew began to intentionally carve out time each week for rest, setting boundaries around his work so that he could fully engage with his loved ones and nurture his relationship with God.

Over time, Andrew's commitment to balance transformed his life. He became a more present husband, a more engaged father, and a more effective leader, not just at work but at home. By honoring the Sabbath and embracing moments of rest, Andrew found the strength to lead with integrity, demonstrating that true success lies not in constant striving, but in honoring God's design for rest, reflection, and meaningful connection.

Old Testament: Exodus 20:8 "Remember the Sabbath day, to keep it holy."

New Testament: Mark 6:31 "And he said to them, 'Come away by yourselves to a desolate place and rest a while.'"

As Christian men striving to balance our professional responsibilities and family commitments, we are reminded in Exodus 20:8 to honor the Sabbath and keep it holy, emphasizing the importance of rest and reflection amidst our busy lives. Similarly, in Mark 6:31, Jesus invites His disciples to retreat and recharge, highlighting that even in our work, we must prioritize time for rejuvenation and connection with loved ones. Let us take these scriptures to heart, intentionally setting aside time each week to disconnect from our professional demands and reconnect with God and our families. In doing so, we cultivate a healthier, more fulfilling life that honors both our commitments and our Creator.

🛠 The Forge Weekly Reflection Sheet

Personal Study & Leadership Accountability Questions

1. Theme in My Life: This week's theme was
"____"

   In my current life, I see this theme at work in the area of:
   "____
   ____"

2. Key Verse Insight: The Scripture that stood out most to me this week was:
   "____
   ____"

3. *Because it reminded/taught/convicted me that:*
   "____
   ____
   ____
   ____"

4. Connection—The story of _________ made me think about:
   "____
   ____"

5. *A similar situation in my life has been:*
   "____
   ____
   ____
   ____"

6. **God's Prompting: One way I feel God is prompting me to grow or change this week is:**

   "_____
   _____
   _____
   _____"

7. **Action Step: As a man of faith and leadership, one practical step I will take this week is:**

   "_____
   _____
   _____
   _____"

8. **Prayer Focus: I sense the need to bring this to God in prayer:**

   "_____
   _____
   _____
   _____"

9. *I also want to lift up these specific people or situations:*

   "_____
   _____
   _____
   _____"

10. **Brotherhood Check-in:**
    One truth I need to share or process with another man is:

    "_____
    _____
    _____
    _____"

11. I plan to connect with: _____ by (day/time): _____

12. Refining at The Forge:
    This week, God is shaping me most in the area of:
    "_____
    _____
    _____
    _____"

13. *I want to remain faithful in this process by:*
    "_____
    _____
    _____
    _____"

Week 23
Supportive Partnership in Marriage

Encouraging and supporting one's spouse in their individual gifts and calling.

A Supportive Partnership

Joshua and Sarah had been married for over a decade, and they shared a deep love and mutual respect. While Joshua thrived in his career, Sarah had recently felt a stirring in her heart to pursue something new—starting her own home-based bakery. She had always loved baking, and friends frequently praised her creations, but taking the leap from hobby to business seemed daunting. Sarah hesitated, worried about balancing this dream with her responsibilities as a wife and mother.

One evening, as they sat together after dinner, Sarah nervously shared her desire with Joshua. "I've been thinking about starting a bakery from home," she confessed. "I know it's a lot, and I don't want to add stress, but it's something I feel called to do."

Joshua listened intently, recalling Ecclesiastes 4:9: "Two are better than one, because they have a good reward for their toil." He understood that their marriage was about working together, supporting each other's dreams and callings. In this moment, he saw an opportunity to be the supportive partner Sarah needed.

"I think that's a great idea," Joshua said, his voice filled with encouragement. "You have an incredible gift, and I've seen how happy baking makes you. Let's figure out how we can make this work together."

Sarah's face lit up, relieved and grateful for Joshua's support. Joshua spent the next few weeks helping her set up the kitchen, researching business tips, and even creating a simple website to showcase her products. He took on extra household chores, giving Sarah the space and time she needed to perfect her recipes and focus on her new venture.

As Sarah's bakery started to gain traction, there were long days filled with early mornings and late nights. Joshua stepped in wherever he could, understanding that supporting Sarah meant more than just words—it meant action. He remembered 1 Peter 3:7: "Likewise, husbands, live with your wives in an understanding way..." Joshua knew that his role was to be Sarah's partner, not just in the easy moments but in the challenging ones too.

One Saturday, Sarah received a large order that overwhelmed her. As she frantically worked, the stress began to show. Sensing her frustration, Joshua put on an apron and joined her in the kitchen, following her instructions to help finish the order on time. Together, they laughed, made a mess, and turned what could have been a stressful experience into a bonding moment.

That night, after the orders were delivered and the kitchen was clean, Sarah hugged Joshua tightly. "I couldn't do this without you," she said, tears of gratitude in her eyes.

Joshua smiled, grateful for the chance to walk alongside Sarah in her journey. "We're in this together," he replied. "Your dreams are my dreams too."

Through this experience, Joshua learned that being a supportive partner wasn't just about encouraging Sarah's gifts—it was about creating a space where her talents could shine. By living out the principles of Ecclesiastes 4:9 and 1 Peter 3:7, he demonstrated the strength found in partnership and the power of understanding and support.

Joshua's commitment to fostering Sarah's calling brought them closer together, reinforcing the idea that a marriage thrives when both partners champion each other's goals. Their home became a place where mutual respect and encouragement were the foundation, allowing both Joshua and Sarah to pursue God's purpose for their lives.

Together, they embodied a supportive partnership, reflecting Christ's love and grace in their marriage. Joshua's willingness to stand beside Sarah, not just in words but in action, created a legacy of love and encouragement that would inspire not only their family but also those around them.

> Old Testament: Ecclesiastes 4:9 "Two are better than one, because they have a good reward for their toil."
>
> New Testament: 1 Peter 3:7 "Likewise, husbands, live with your wives in an understanding way...

As Christian men, we are called to be supportive partners in our marriages, recognizing that, as Ecclesiastes 4:9 reminds us, "Two are better than one, because they have a good reward for their toil." This verse highlights the strength found in partnership, urging us to encourage our wives in their unique gifts and callings. In 1 Peter 3:7, we are instructed to live with our wives in an understanding way, which calls us to listen, nurture, and uplift them. Let us embrace our roles as champions of our spouses, fostering an environment where their talents can flourish, and together we can fulfill God's purpose for our lives. In doing so, we reflect His love and grace within our homes, creating a legacy of mutual support and encouragement.

✖ The Forge Weekly Reflection Sheet

Personal Study & Leadership Accountability Questions

1. **Theme in My Life: This week's theme was**
   "_____"
   In my current life, I see this theme at work in the area of:
   "_____
   _____"

2. **Key Verse Insight: The Scripture that stood out most to me this week was:**
   "_____
   _____"

3. *Because it reminded/taught/convicted me that:*
   "_____
   _____
   _____
   _____"

4. *Connection—The story of _____ made me think about:*
   "_____
   _____"

5. *A similar situation in my life has been:*
   "_____
   _____
   _____
   _____"

6. **God's Prompting: One way I feel God is prompting me to grow or change this week is:**
   " _____
   _____
   _____
   _____ "

7. **Action Step: As a man of faith and leadership, one practical step I will take this week is:**
   " _____
   _____
   _____
   _____ "

8. **Prayer Focus: I sense the need to bring this to God in prayer:**
   " _____
   _____
   _____
   _____ "

9. *I also want to lift up these specific people or situations:*
   " _____
   _____
   _____
   _____ "

10. **Brotherhood Check-in:**
    One truth I need to share or process with another man is:
    " _____
    _____
    _____
    _____ "

11. I plan to connect with: _____ by (day/time): _____

12. Refining at The Forge:
    This week, God is shaping me most in the area of:
    "_____
    _____
    _____
    _____"

13. *I want to remain faithful in this process by:*
    "_____
    _____
    _____
    _____"

Week 24
Leadership in Worship

Leading by example in worship, encouraging others to seek God through praise and prayer.

Leading in Worship with Joy

Kenneth had always been a quiet man, steady and dependable in his roles as a husband, father, and church member. But when it came to worship, he often found himself holding back, content to stand in the background. He loved God deeply but was hesitant to express his praise openly, worried about what others might think. One Sunday, his church announced a special family worship night, and his young daughter, Emma, excitedly tugged on his sleeve. "Daddy, will you sing with us?"

That question lingered with Kenneth. He remembered Psalm 100:2: "Serve the Lord with gladness! Come into his presence with singing!" He knew that worship was more than just a personal moment—it was an opportunity to lead his family and his church community into God's presence. But stepping out of his comfort zone felt intimidating.

On the night of the event, Kenneth watched as his church gathered in the sanctuary, filled with families ready to worship together. The worship team began to play, and the room filled with voices lifting up praise. Emma looked up at him with hopeful eyes, and Kenneth felt a stirring in his heart. He realized that his worship wasn't just for himself—it was a chance to set an example for his daughter and everyone around him.

Inspired by Colossians 3:16, which says, "Let the word of Christ dwell in you richly, teaching and admonishing one another in all wisdom...," Kenneth knew that his worship could encourage others, not through perfection, but through authenticity. He took a deep breath, raised his hands, and began to sing with all his heart. For the first time, he wasn't worried about how he looked or sounded—he was fully focused on God.

As Kenneth sang, something beautiful happened. Emma's voice grew louder and more confident beside him, and soon, their whole family was caught up in the joy of worship. Kenneth noticed others around him doing the same—parents singing with their children, friends clapping along, and a sense of unity and joy spreading throughout the room.

At one point, the worship leader stepped back from the microphone, letting the congregation's voices fill the space. Kenneth looked around and saw people worshiping freely, inspired by the collective praise. Tears welled in his eyes as he felt the presence of God moving among them, connecting their hearts in a powerful way.

After the service, several church members approached Kenneth, thanking him for his openness in worship. "Seeing you worship encouraged me to let go and do the same," one man said. Kenneth realized that his small act of stepping forward in worship had a ripple effect, creating an atmosphere where others felt free to seek God with their whole hearts.

From that night on, Kenneth made it a point to lead by example in worship, both at church and at home. He began incorporating worship music into their family routines, turning everyday moments into opportunities to praise God together. Whether singing in the car, praying before meals, or sharing Scripture, Kenneth led his family with a heart of worship, showing them that seeking God was not just a Sunday activity but a way of life.

Kenneth's willingness to embrace his role as a leader in worship transformed not only his relationship with God but also his family's faith. By serving the Lord with gladness and letting the word of Christ dwell richly in his life, Kenneth became a beacon of encouragement in his church, fostering a community that sought God through praise and prayer.

His actions taught others that worship was not about performance but about connection—drawing near to God and inviting those around us to do the same. Through his example, Kenneth cultivated a spirit of worship that went beyond words, creating a lasting impact that echoed the joy and reverence of Psalm 100:2, inspiring everyone who witnessed his authentic praise.

> Old Testament: Psalm 100:2 "Serve the Lord with gladness! Come into his presence with singing!"
>
> New Testament: Colossians 3:16 "Let the word of Christ dwell in you richly, teaching and admonishing one another in all wisdom..."

As Christian men, we are called to lead by example in our worship, embodying the joy and reverence outlined in Psalm 100:2: "Serve the Lord with gladness! Come into his presence with singing!" Our worship is not just a personal expression; it is an invitation for others to seek God through our praise and prayer. Colossians 3:16 encourages us to let the word of Christ dwell in us richly, teaching and admonishing one another in wisdom. Let us commit to being authentic leaders in worship,

The Forge

demonstrating our love for God in both song and action. By cultivating a heart of praise and inviting others into that space, we create a community that seeks the Lord together, fostering an environment where His presence can be felt and experienced.

Men's Leadership Devotional 201

✖ The Forge Weekly Reflection Sheet

Personal Study & Leadership Accountability Questions

1. **Theme in My Life: This week's theme was**
   "_____"
   In my current life, I see this theme at work in the area of:
   "_____
   _____"

2. **Key Verse Insight: The Scripture that stood out most to me this week was:**
   "_____
   _____"

3. *Because it reminded/taught/convicted me that:*
   "_____
   _____
   _____"

4. **Connection—The story of _____ made me think about:**
   "_____
   _____"

5. *A similar situation in my life has been:*
   "_____
   _____
   _____"

6. **God's Prompting: One way I feel God is prompting me to grow or change this week is:**
   "_____
   _____
   _____
   _____"

7. **Action Step: As a man of faith and leadership, one practical step I will take this week is:**
   "_____
   _____
   _____
   _____"

8. **Prayer Focus: I sense the need to bring this to God in prayer:**
   "_____
   _____
   _____
   _____"

9. *I also want to lift up these specific people or situations:*
   "_____
   _____
   _____
   _____"

10. **Brotherhood Check-in:**
    One truth I need to share or process with another man is:
    "_____
    _____
    _____
    _____"

11. I plan to connect with: _____ by (day/time): _____

12. Refining at The Forge:
    This week, God is shaping me most in the area of:
    "_____
    _____
    _____
    _____"

13. *I want to remain faithful in this process by:*
    "_____
    _____
    _____
    _____"

Week 25
Overcoming Temptation

Equipping oneself to resist temptation, demonstrating reliance on God's strength.

Standing Firm Against Temptation

Ethan was a dedicated father, husband, and leader at his church, but like everyone, he faced his own battles. Lately, stress at work and the pressures of life had been weighing heavily on him. One evening, after a particularly difficult day, Ethan found himself alone at home, scrolling through his phone. Temptation crept in—a familiar urge to escape into the comfort of unhealthy habits he thought he had left behind.

As his finger hovered over a website he knew he shouldn't visit, Ethan felt the pull of shame and defeat. But then, 1 Corinthians 10:13 came to his mind: "No temptation has overtaken you that is not common to man. God is faithful, and he will not let you be tempted beyond your ability…" Ethan realized he wasn't facing this struggle alone. God was with him, providing a way out, even when it felt impossible.

Ethan quickly put his phone down and walked to his study, where he kept his Bible. He opened it, desperately seeking the strength that had been promised to him. His eyes fell on James 1:12: "Blessed is the man who remains steadfast under trial, for when he has stood the test he will receive the crown of life…" Ethan knew that giving in would only bring temporary relief but standing firm would lead to true victory.

Determined to resist, Ethan knelt beside his chair and prayed. "Lord, I'm struggling, but I know You are stronger than this temptation. Help me stay true to You. I need Your strength right now." As he prayed, Ethan felt a wave of peace and clarity wash over him. He realized that God was not asking him to fight this battle alone—He was there, providing the strength Ethan needed to remain steadfast.

Ian knew he needed more than just a moment of prayer; he needed accountability. He picked up his phone, but this time, he reached out to his friend and mentor, Tom, who had been a spiritual guide for him. "Hey Tom, I'm struggling tonight. Can you pray with me?"

Tom responded immediately, offering encouragement and reminding Ian of God's promises. They prayed together, and Tom shared practical advice on how to guard his heart and mind, emphasizing the importance of setting boundaries and staying connected to God's Word. Ian felt a renewed sense of determination, knowing he wasn't fighting alone.

Over the next few weeks, Ian continued to lean on Scripture and prayer, building new habits that kept him grounded. He began each day with a quiet time, reflecting on verses that reminded him of God's strength. He also committed to weekly check-ins with Tom, creating a support system that kept him accountable and encouraged.

One afternoon, Ian found himself in another stressful situation, but this time, instead of turning to old habits, he took a moment to pray and recall the promises of 1 Corinthians 10:13. He resisted the temptation, and though the battle was not easy, he felt a deep sense of victory. He had stood firm, not in his own strength but in God's.

Ethan's journey taught him that overcoming temptation was not about willpower alone but about relying on God's faithfulness and equipping himself with the right tools—prayer, Scripture, and community. Each time he chose to stand firm, he felt himself growing stronger, and his faith deepened.

Through his struggles, Ian became a testament to the truth of James 1:12, experiencing the blessing of steadfastness. He shared his journey openly with other men in his church, encouraging them to find strength in God when faced with their own temptations. Ethan's vulnerability and determination inspired others to seek God's help in their battles, creating a ripple effect of accountability and support.

Ethan's story was a reminder that no temptation is insurmountable when we rely on God's strength. By standing firm and remaining steadfast, he reflected the victory of Christ in his life, proving that even in our weakest moments, God is faithful to provide the way out and lead us to the crown of life.

> Old Testament: 1 Corinthians 10:13 "No temptation has overtaken you that is not common to man. God is faithful, and he will not let you be tempted beyond your ability..."
>
> New Testament: James 1:12 "Blessed is the man who remains steadfast under trial, for when he has stood the test he will receive the crown of life..."

As Christian men, we face temptations that challenge our faith and integrity, but we can draw strength from the promise in 1 Corinthians 10:13, which reassures us that

208 The Forge

"God is faithful, and he will not let you be tempted beyond your ability." This reminds us that every struggle we encounter is not unique, and we are never alone in our battles. In James 1:12, we learn that "Blessed is the man who remains steadfast under trial," emphasizing the importance of perseverance in the face of temptation. Let us equip ourselves with prayer, Scripture, and accountability, relying on God's strength to overcome challenges. By standing firm, we not only grow in faith but also receive the crown of life promised to those who remain steadfast, reflecting the victory of Christ in our lives.

Men's Leadership Devotional 209

🛠 The Forge Weekly Reflection Sheet

Personal Study & Leadership Accountability Questions

1. **Theme in My Life: This week's theme was**
   " _____ "

   In my current life, I see this theme at work in the area of:
   " _____
   _____ "

2. **Key Verse Insight: The Scripture that stood out most to me this week was:**
   " _____
   _____ "

3. *Because it reminded/taught/convicted me that:*
   " _____
   _____
   _____
   _____ "

4. **Connection—The story of _____ made me think about:**
   " _____
   _____ "

5. *A similar situation in my life has been:*
   " _____
   _____
   _____
   _____ "

6. **God's Prompting: One way I feel God is prompting me to grow or change this week is:**
   " _____
   _____
   _____
   _____ "

7. **Action Step: As a man of faith and leadership, one practical step I will take this week is:**
   " _____
   _____
   _____
   _____ "

8. **Prayer Focus: I sense the need to bring this to God in prayer:**
   " _____
   _____
   _____
   _____ "

9. *I also want to lift up these specific people or situations:*
   " _____
   _____
   _____
   _____ "

10. **Brotherhood Check-in:**
    One truth I need to share or process with another man is:
    " _____
    _____
    _____
    _____ "

11. I plan to connect with: _____ by (day/time): _____

12. Refining at The Forge:
    This week, God is shaping me most in the area of:
    "_____
    _____
    _____
    _____"

13. *I want to remain faithful in this process by:*
    "_____
    _____
    _____
    _____"

Week 26
Fostering a Culture of Honor

Creating an environment where respect and honor are foundational within relationships.

Creating a Culture of Honor

Jake was the head coach of the local high school basketball team, a role he took seriously not just for the sake of winning games, but for mentoring young men. Over the years, Jake had built a solid team, but lately, he'd noticed something troubling—a growing tension among the players. The younger athletes felt overlooked, the seniors were demanding more respect, and a general sense of competition off the court was eroding the team's unity.

One evening after practice, Jake sat in his office, reflecting on how to address the issue. He thought of Romans 12:10: "Love one another with brotherly affection. Outdo one another in showing honor." Jake realized that the problem wasn't just about skill or strategy—it was about creating a culture of honor, where each player felt respected and valued, regardless of their role.

The next day, Jake called a team meeting. He started by sharing his concerns and reading Romans 12:10 aloud. "This verse isn't just for church—it's for us, right here, right now. We need to learn to honor each other, not just as teammates but as brothers."

Jake then introduced a new tradition: every week, each player would take a turn recognizing another teammate. It didn't matter if the recognition was for a great play, helping a fellow student with homework, or simply showing up with a positive attitude. The point was to foster an environment of respect and appreciation.

During the first week, a senior captain, Mark, stood up and surprised everyone by honoring a freshman, Chris, who had been quietly giving his all in practice. "Chris, you push hard every day, and I see how you hustle even when no one's watching. You're the kind of player we need more of on this team." Chris beamed, clearly moved by the unexpected praise.

The tradition quickly took root. The players began to look for ways to honor each other, not just in the weekly meetings but in daily interactions—helping each other with drills, cheering louder for one another during games, and offering words of encouragement instead of criticism. The atmosphere shifted, and the team's unity grew stronger.

Jake also made it a point to publicly honor his assistant coaches and staff, drawing from 1 Timothy 5:17: "Let the elders who rule well be considered worthy of double honor..." He recognized their hard work and dedication, ensuring the players knew that the success of the team was a collective effort. This gesture of respect trickled down, as players began to show gratitude for those who often worked behind the scenes.

By the end of the season, the team was not only winning games but also winning each other's respect. One night, after a particularly tough game, Jake watched with pride as the players, sweaty and tired, took time to congratulate each other, lifting up the youngest and newest members for their contributions. The culture of honor had transformed the team from a group of individuals into a true family.

Jake's intentionality in fostering a culture of honor had a lasting impact. The players learned that honoring each other wasn't just about recognition; it was about seeing the value in everyone and celebrating it. It created a space where each person felt seen, respected, and inspired to do their best—not just for themselves but for the team.

Through this journey, Jake saw the profound truth of Romans 12:10 and 1 Timothy 5:17 in action. By outdoing one another in showing honor, they reflected Christ's love and built relationships that went beyond the court. Jake's leadership demonstrated that when honor and respect are foundational, it doesn't just change a team—it changes hearts and lives.

In creating a culture of honor, Jake modeled the kind of leadership that inspired not just better players but better men, teaching them that respect and dignity are at the heart of every successful relationship, both on and off the court.

> Old Testament: Romans 12:10 "Love one another with brotherly affection. Outdo one another in showing honor."
>
> New Testament: 1 Timothy 5:17 "Let the elders who rule well be considered worthy of double honor…"

As Christian men, we are called to foster a culture of honor in our relationships, where respect and affection are foundational. Romans 12:10 encourages us to "love one another with brotherly affection" and to "outdo one another in showing honor." This challenges us to prioritize the dignity of others, actively seeking ways to uplift and celebrate those around us. Additionally, 1 Timothy 5:17

The Forge

reminds us to give double honor to those who lead well, recognizing the hard work and sacrifices they make for our community. By embodying a spirit of honor, we create an environment where everyone feels valued and respected, reflecting Christ's love in our interactions. Let us strive to be men who not only show honor but inspire it in others, building relationships that reflect the heart of God.

🛠 The Forge Weekly Reflection Sheet

Personal Study & Leadership Accountability Questions

1. **Theme in My Life: This week's theme was**
   "____"
   In my current life, I see this theme at work in the area of:
   "____
   ____"

2. **Key Verse Insight: The Scripture that stood out most to me this week was:**
   "____
   ____"

3. ***Because it reminded/taught/convicted me that:***
   "____
   ____
   ____
   ____"

4. **Connection—The story of _________ made me think about:**
   "____
   ____"

5. ***A similar situation in my life has been:***
   "____
   ____
   ____
   ____"

6. **God's Prompting:** One way I feel God is prompting me to grow or change this week is:
   "_____
   _____
   _____
   _____"

7. **Action Step:** As a man of faith and leadership, one practical step I will take this week is:
   "_____
   _____
   _____
   _____"

8. **Prayer Focus:** I sense the need to bring this to God in prayer:
   "_____
   _____
   _____
   _____"

9. *I also want to lift up these specific people or situations:*
   "_____
   _____
   _____
   _____"

10. **Brotherhood Check-in:**
    One truth I need to share or process with another man is:
    "_____
    _____
    _____
    _____"

11. I plan to connect with: _____ by (day/time): _____

12. **Refining at The Forge:**
   This week, God is shaping me most in the area of:
   "_____
   _____
   _____
   _____"

13. *I want to remain faithful in this process by:*
   "_____
   _____
   _____
   _____"

Week 27
Listening and Communication

Practicing active listening and open communication, fostering healthy dialogues.

The Power of Listening

Joe was known as a man of action—decisive, quick to respond, and always ready to fix problems. At work, this made him an effective leader, but at home, his tendency to jump in with answers often left his wife, Jenna, and teenage son, Tyler, feeling unheard. One evening, after a long day, Joe noticed that Tyler seemed withdrawn, staring at his phone in silence. Sensing something was wrong, Joe asked, "What's going on, Tyler? You've been quiet all night."

Tyler hesitated but finally said, "I had a rough day at school." Ben, eager to help, immediately launched into advice. "You've got to stand up for yourself, buddy. If someone's giving you trouble, you can't just back down. You need to…"

Before Joe could finish, Tyler stood up abruptly. "You don't get it, Dad!" he said, frustration bubbling over. "You never listen. You just tell me what to do." He stormed off to his room, leaving Joe stunned and hurt.

Joe sat down, his mind replaying the moment. He thought of Proverbs 18:13: "If one gives an answer before he hears, it is his folly and shame." He realized that he hadn't really listened to Tyler's heart—he had been more focused on offering solutions than understanding the problem. Joe knew that to truly connect with his son, he needed to change his approach.

The next morning, Joe remembered James 1:19: "Let every person be quick to hear, slow to speak, slow to anger." He decided to try again, this time with a different mindset. He knocked on Tyler's door and sat down beside him, taking a deep breath. "Tyler, I'm sorry for last night. I want to listen. Can you tell me what's really going on?"

Tyler hesitated, then began to share about a conflict with friends that had been weighing heavily on him. Joe listened intently, resisting the urge to interrupt or fix. He nodded, validating Tyler's feelings and letting him vent his frustrations. As Tyler talked, Joe realized that his son wasn't looking for answers—he just needed to be heard and understood.

When Tyler finished, Joe simply said, "I'm sorry you're going through this. That sounds really tough." The weight of the conversation lifted as Tyler saw his dad's genuine concern. "Thanks, Dad. I just needed to get it off my chest."

From that day on, Joe committed to practicing active listening, not just with Tyler but with Jenna and others in his life. He made a conscious effort to pause, listen fully, and respond with empathy rather than jumping to conclusions. This shift in his communication style brought a new level of closeness to his relationships, allowing for deeper, more meaningful dialogues.

At work, Joe noticed the change, too. By listening more and speaking less, he fostered a culture of openness among his team. Colleagues felt more comfortable sharing their ideas and concerns, knowing they had a leader who valued their input.

One evening, Jenna approached Ben, smiling. "I've noticed a difference in how you've been with Tyler lately. He really feels heard by you." Joe nodded, grateful for the change that God was working in him. He realized that the principles of Proverbs 18:13 and James 1:19 weren't just about communication—they were about honoring others, creating a space where every voice mattered.

Through his journey of learning to listen, Joe discovered that true leadership didn't always mean having the right answers but having the patience to hear and the humility to understand. By being quick to listen and slow to speak, he strengthened his connections with his family and those around him, reflecting Christ's love through every conversation.

Ben's story became a testament to the power of active listening and open communication. He saw that when we take the time to truly hear others, we build trust, foster respect, and create relationships that are not just stronger but filled with grace and understanding.

> Old Testament: Proverbs 18:13 "If one gives an answer before he hears, it is his folly and shame."
>
> New Testament: James 1:19 "Know this, my beloved brothers: let every person be quick to hear, slow to speak, slow to anger."

As Christian men, we are called to cultivate the art of listening and communication, which are vital for building healthy relationships. Proverbs 18:13 warns us that "if one gives an answer before he hears, it is his folly and shame," reminding us of the importance of truly understanding others before responding. In James 1:19, we are encouraged to be "quick to hear, slow to speak, slow to anger," guiding us to approach conversations with patience and openness. By practicing active listening, we honor those we engage with and create a safe space for meaningful dialogue. Let us commit to fostering an environment where every voice is valued and heard, reflecting the love and wisdom of Christ in our interactions and strengthening our relationships in the process.

⚒ The Forge Weekly Reflection Sheet

Personal Study & Leadership Accountability Questions

1. **Theme in My Life: This week's theme was**
   "_____"

   In my current life, I see this theme at work in the area of:
   "_____
   _____"

2. **Key Verse Insight: The Scripture that stood out most to me this week was:**
   "_____
   _____"

3. *Because it reminded/taught/convicted me that:*
   "_____
   _____
   _____
   _____"

4. **Connection—The story of _____ made me think about:**
   "_____
   _____"

5. *A similar situation in my life has been:*
   "_____
   _____
   _____
   _____"

6. **God's Prompting: One way I feel God is prompting me to grow or change this week is:**
   "_____
   _____
   _____
   _____"

7. **Action Step: As a man of faith and leadership, one practical step I will take this week is:**
   "_____
   _____
   _____
   _____"

8. **Prayer Focus: I sense the need to bring this to God in prayer:**
   "_____
   _____
   _____
   _____"

9. *I also want to lift up these specific people or situations:*
   "_____
   _____
   _____
   _____"

10. **Brotherhood Check-in:**
    One truth I need to share or process with another man is:
    "_____
    _____
    _____
    _____"

11. I plan to connect with: _____ by (day/time): _____

12. Refining at The Forge:
This week, God is shaping me most in the area of:
"_____
_____
_____
_____"

13. *I want to remain faithful in this process by:*
"_____
_____
_____
_____"

Week 28
Embracing Diversity

Recognizing and celebrating the diversity within the body of Christ and the broader community.

Embracing Diversity in Community

Marcus was an elder at his local church, a place he had attended for years and where he felt comfortable and connected. However, lately, he noticed that the congregation was becoming increasingly diverse—people from different backgrounds, cultures, and walks of life were joining, and the church was beginning to look more like the broader community around it. Some welcomed the change, but others struggled with the differences, unsure of how to connect with those who didn't look, speak, or worship quite like they did.

One Sunday, the pastor invited several new members to share their testimonies. Among them was Rosa, a recent immigrant who spoke about her journey to the U.S. and how she found comfort in the church despite language barriers. Then came Samir, a young man from the Middle East who had recently come to faith and was excited to be part of a community that embraced him. As Marcus listened, he was struck by the beauty of their stories—each one a unique reflection of God's work.

That night, Marcus reflected on Genesis 1:27: "So God created man in his own image, in the image of God he created him; male and female he created them." He realized that every person, regardless of their background, was a reflection of God's image, carrying a piece of His creativity, love, and purpose. Marcus felt convicted that the church wasn't just a place for those who looked and thought like him—it was a home for everyone, a small glimpse of heaven.

Inspired by Revelation 7:9, which describes a great multitude from every nation, tribe, and language worshiping together, Marcus felt compelled to do more than just welcome diversity; he wanted to actively embrace it. The next Sunday, he invited Rosa and her family over for lunch after church, eager to learn more about their culture and experience. He asked Samir to coffee, listening as Samir shared his journey of faith and the challenges of navigating a new community.

Through these simple acts of hospitality, Marcus found his own perspective widening. He began to see the church as a living tapestry, each person contributing a unique thread that made the community richer and more vibrant. He encouraged the church leadership to integrate diverse elements into their worship services, from incorporating songs in different languages to celebrating cultural heritage days that highlighted the various backgrounds within their congregation.

As the months passed, the church became a true reflection of the kingdom of God—an inclusive space where people of all nations, tribes, and languages felt seen, heard, and valued. Marcus noticed how this celebration of diversity strengthened their community, breaking down walls of misunderstanding and replacing them with bridges of respect and love.

One evening, during a potluck that featured foods from around the world, Marcus looked around the room filled with laughter, shared stories, and a sense of unity. He felt a deep gratitude for the diverse body of Christ gathered before him. They were no longer just a congregation—they were a family, brought together by the love of God that transcended every barrier.

Through his journey of embracing diversity, Marcus learned that every individual, no matter their background, was a vital part of God's design. By honoring and celebrating the differences among them, they were not only reflecting the image of God but also glimpsing the heavenly vision painted in Revelation 7:9.

Marcus's commitment to fostering a culture of inclusivity transformed his church, creating a welcoming environment that mirrored the heart of God. His efforts inspired others to reach out, to listen, and to value the unique stories each person brought. The church became a powerful testimony of unity in diversity, a living witness of what it means to be one body in Christ, celebrating the beautiful mosaic of humanity that God has crafted.

> Old Testament: Genesis 1:27 "So God created man in his own image, in the image of God he created him; male and female he created them."
>
> New Testament: Revelation 7:9 "After this I looked, and behold, a great multitude that no one could number, from every nation, from all tribes and peoples and languages..."

As Christian men, we are called to embrace and celebrate the rich diversity within the body of Christ and our broader community. Genesis 1:27 reminds us that we are all created in the image of God, each reflecting unique facets of His creativity and love—"male and female He created them." This foundational truth invites us to appreciate the distinct backgrounds, perspectives, and gifts that every individual brings. Revelation 7:9 paints a beautiful picture of heaven, where a multitude from "every nation, from all tribes and peoples and languages" gathers in unity. Let us commit to fostering an inclusive spirit, honoring our differences while recognizing our shared identity in Christ. By doing so, we reflect God's kingdom on earth, creating a community that celebrates and values the beautiful tapestry of humanity.

Men's Leadership Devotional 233

🛠 The Forge Weekly Reflection Sheet

Personal Study & Leadership Accountability Questions

1. **Theme in My Life: This week's theme was**
   " _____ "
   In my current life, I see this theme at work in the area of:
   " _____
   _____ "

2. **Key Verse Insight: The Scripture that stood out most to me this week was:**
   " _____
   _____ "

3. *Because it reminded/taught/convicted me that:*
   " _____
   _____
   _____
   _____ "

4. **Connection—The story of _____ made me think about:**
   " _____
   _____ "

5. *A similar situation in my life has been:*
   " _____
   _____
   _____ "

6. **God's Prompting:** One way I feel God is prompting me to grow or change this week is:

   "_____
   _____
   _____
   _____"

7. **Action Step:** As a man of faith and leadership, one practical step I will take this week is:

   "_____
   _____
   _____
   _____"

8. **Prayer Focus:** I sense the need to bring this to God in prayer:

   "_____
   _____
   _____
   _____"

9. *I also want to lift up these specific people or situations:*

   "_____
   _____
   _____
   _____"

10. **Brotherhood Check-in:**
    One truth I need to share or process with another man is:

    "_____
    _____
    _____
    _____"

11. I plan to connect with: _____ by (day/time): _____

12. **Refining at The Forge:**
    This week, God is shaping me most in the area of:
    "_____
    _____
    _____
    _____"

13. *I want to remain faithful in this process by:*
    "_____
    _____
    _____
    _____"

Week 29
Service to the Vulnerable

Advocating for and serving the marginalized and vulnerable in society.

Serving the Vulnerable with Compassion

Brian was a dedicated businessman and father, known for his commitment to his church and family. But beyond his comfortable routine, Brian was often unaware of the struggles that lay just beyond his community. One evening, during a church meeting, a guest speaker from a local shelter shared stories of the homeless and vulnerable in their city—individuals who had lost jobs, families who couldn't make ends meet, and teens who had been abandoned. As Brian listened, he felt a stirring in his heart that he couldn't ignore.

The speaker concluded by quoting Proverbs 31:8-9: "Open your mouth for the mute, for the rights of all who are destitute. Open your mouth, judge righteously, defend the rights of the poor and needy." Brian realized that his role as a Christian man extended beyond his immediate circle; he was called to be an advocate for those who had no voice, to stand up for the marginalized and vulnerable.

That week, Brian decided to visit the shelter with his teenage son, Luke, wanting to see firsthand the needs of the community. As they served meals and listened to the stories of those they met, Brian was deeply moved. One conversation with a young mother struggling to provide for her children particularly touched him. "I'm just trying to get back on my feet," she said, her voice tinged with both hope and weariness.

Brian thought of Matthew 25:40: "Truly, I say to you, as you did it to one of the least of these my brothers, you did it to me." He realized that every act of kindness he extended to these individuals was a service to Christ Himself. Brian knew he had to do more than just serve a meal—he needed to be an advocate and a supporter.

Motivated by this new perspective, Brian began to organize monthly volunteer days at the shelter, rallying his friends, family, and church members to get involved. He also used his business connections to help those in need find jobs, offering coaching sessions on resume writing and interview skills. Brian became a familiar face at the shelter, not just as a helper but as a friend who genuinely cared about the people he met.

Through his consistent presence and advocacy, Brian's efforts began to make a tangible difference. He watched as individuals he had helped found work, secured housing, and slowly rebuilt their lives. One day, the young mother he had met during his first visit approached him with tears in her eyes. "Thank you for believing in me," she said. "I have a job now, and things are finally turning around."

Brian's heart swelled with gratitude, knowing that his actions were a reflection of Christ's call to serve the least of these. He had learned that serving the vulnerable was not about charity—it was about justice, compassion, and dignity. By opening his heart and hands, Brian had become a living example of Proverbs 31:8-9, using his voice and resources to lift up those who needed it most.

Luke, inspired by his father's dedication, began organizing his own service projects with his school friends, extending the impact of their efforts even further. Brian realized that his commitment to serving the vulnerable was not only transforming lives but also setting a powerful example for the next generation.

Brian's journey taught him that true leadership meant stepping out of his comfort zone and into the places where God's love was needed most. By embracing his calling to serve and advocate, he saw how one person's actions could ripple out to bring hope, dignity, and change to those often overlooked.

Through his advocacy and service, Brian not only reflected the heart of Christ but also created a culture of compassion within his community. He demonstrated that when we serve the least among us, we are truly serving the King, making a difference that echoes far beyond the walls of the shelter and into eternity.

> Old Testament: Proverbs 31:89 "Open your mouth for the mute, for the rights of all who are destitute. Open your mouth, judge righteously, defend the rights of the poor and needy."
>
> New Testament: Matthew 25:40 "And the King will answer them, 'Truly, I say to you, as you did it to one of the least of these my brothers, you did it to me.'"

As Christian men, we are called to advocate for and serve the marginalized and vulnerable in our society, reflecting the heart of God in our actions. Proverbs 31:8-9 urges us to "open your mouth for the mute, for the rights of all who are destitute," highlighting our responsibility to speak up for those who cannot advocate for themselves and to judge righteously. Similarly, Matthew 25:40 reminds us that when we serve "one of the least of these," we are, in fact, serving Christ Himself. Let us embrace this calling with humility and compassion, actively seeking opportunities to support those in need. By embodying Christ's love and justice, we can make a tangible difference in the lives of the vulnerable, transforming our communities and reflecting His grace to the world.

⚒ The Forge Weekly Reflection Sheet

Personal Study & Leadership Accountability Questions

1. **Theme in My Life: This week's theme was**
   "_____"
   In my current life, I see this theme at work in the area of:
   "_____
   _____"

2. **Key Verse Insight: The Scripture that stood out most to me this week was:**
   "_____
   _____"

3. *Because it reminded/taught/convicted me that:*
   "_____
   _____
   _____
   _____"

4. **Connection—The story of _____ made me think about:**
   "_____
   _____"

5. *A similar situation in my life has been:*
   "_____
   _____
   _____
   _____"

6. **God's Prompting: One way I feel God is prompting me to grow or change this week is:**
   "_____
   _____
   _____
   _____"

7. **Action Step: As a man of faith and leadership, one practical step I will take this week is:**
   "_____
   _____
   _____
   _____"

8. **Prayer Focus: I sense the need to bring this to God in prayer:**
   "_____
   _____
   _____
   _____"

9. *I also want to lift up these specific people or situations:*
   "_____
   _____
   _____
   _____"

10. **Brotherhood Check-in:**
    One truth I need to share or process with another man is:
    "_____
    _____
    _____
    _____"

11. I plan to connect with: _____ by (day/time): _____

12. **Refining at The Forge:**
    This week, God is shaping me most in the area of:
    "_____
    _____
    _____
    _____"

13. *I want to remain faithful in this process by:*
    "_____
    _____
    _____
    _____"

Week 30
Resilience in Leadership

Developing resilience to face challenges with faith and perseverance.

Resilient Leadership in the Face of Adversity

Daniel was a dedicated leader in his community, running a nonprofit that provided mentorship and resources for at-risk youth. The organization had grown rapidly, but with that growth came new challenges—financial pressures, staffing shortages, and constant scrutiny from those who doubted the mission. There were days when it felt like the weight of responsibility was too much, and Daniel wondered if all his efforts would be enough to keep the organization afloat.

One afternoon, Daniel received a letter from a major donor announcing they were pulling their support due to financial restructuring. It was a devastating blow; without this funding, critical programs would be cut, and the kids who relied on them would be left without the guidance they desperately needed. The news spread quickly, and Daniel felt the eyes of his staff and board members on him, waiting to see how he would respond.

Sitting in his office, Daniel opened his Bible, searching for comfort and direction. He found himself reading Nehemiah 6:9: "For they all wanted to frighten us, thinking, 'Their hands will drop from the work, and it will not be done.' But now, O God, strengthen my hands."

246 The Forge

Daniel resonated deeply with Nehemiah's prayer. He knew that the challenges before him were more than just financial—they were spiritual battles meant to sow fear and doubt.

Determined not to let adversity derail their mission, Daniel prayed, "Lord, I need Your strength. Help me to keep going, even when it feels impossible." He rose from his desk with a renewed sense of purpose, knowing that his strength didn't come from himself but from God.

Inspired by Romans 5:3-4—"we rejoice in our sufferings, knowing that suffering produces endurance"—Daniel decided to reframe the crisis as an opportunity for growth. He called an emergency meeting with his team, not to dwell on the loss but to brainstorm creative solutions. "We're going to get through this," he said confidently. "This setback doesn't define us. It's our chance to show what we're made of."

Together, they developed new fundraising strategies, reached out to community partners, and tightened their budget. Daniel also took on additional speaking engagements to raise awareness and rally local support. There were long nights, difficult decisions, and moments of doubt, but Daniel kept reminding his team—and himself—that resilience was key.

One evening, after weeks of relentless effort, Daniel received a call from a new donor who had heard about the nonprofit's work and wanted to invest in their mission. The donation was enough to cover the funding gap and even expand some of their most impactful programs. It was a moment of profound relief, but more importantly, it was a testament to the power of perseverance.

The experience strengthened not only Daniel's resolve but also his entire team's faith. They had faced the storm together, leaning on God and one another, and had emerged stronger for it. Daniel used the ordeal as a teaching moment for the youth they served, sharing how resilience in leadership meant not giving up, even when everything seemed stacked against them.

Through the trials, Daniel learned that true leadership is not about avoiding hardship but about facing it with faith. Nehemiah's prayer to "strengthen my hands" became his own anthem, reminding him that every obstacle was an opportunity to grow closer to God and to inspire those around him.

Daniel's resilience became a beacon for his community, demonstrating that the greatest victories often come on the heels of the greatest struggles. His commitment to the mission, despite the challenges, showed that with God's strength, no task is too great and no opposition too fierce.

In the end, Daniel's story was more than just a lesson in perseverance—it was a testament to the faithfulness of God and the power of resilient leadership. He proved that when we face adversity with a steadfast heart, we not only overcome but also inspire others to press on, shining God's light in the darkest moments.

> Old Testament: Nehemiah 6:9 "For they all wanted to frighten us, thinking, 'Their hands will drop from the work, and it will not be done.' But now, O God, strengthen my hands."

> New Testament: Romans 5:34 "Not only that, but we rejoice in our sufferings, knowing that suffering produces endurance..."

As Christian men in leadership, we are called to develop resilience to face challenges with unwavering faith and perseverance. Nehemiah 6:9 highlights the opposition we may encounter, as foes sought to intimidate him, believing that fear would derail his mission. In the face of such trials, Nehemiah boldly prayed, "O God, strengthen my hands," reminding us to seek divine strength in our moments of weakness. Likewise, Romans 5:3-4 teaches us to "rejoice in our sufferings, knowing that suffering produces endurance," affirming that our challenges can lead to greater spiritual maturity. Let us embrace resilience, understanding that each obstacle is an opportunity to grow closer to God and to exemplify His strength in our leadership. By steadfastly moving forward in faith, we can inspire those around us, showing that true leadership shines brightest in adversity.

Men's Leadership Devotional

⚒ The Forge Weekly Reflection Sheet

Personal Study & Leadership Accountability Questions

1. **Theme in My Life: This week's theme was**
   " _____ "

   In my current life, I see this theme at work in the area of:
   " _____
   _____ "

2. **Key Verse Insight: The Scripture that stood out most to me this week was:**
   " _____
   _____ "

3. *Because it reminded/taught/convicted me that:*
   " _____
   _____
   _____
   _____ "

4. **Connection—The story of _____ made me think about:**
   " _____
   _____ "

5. *A similar situation in my life has been:*
   " _____
   _____
   _____
   _____ "

6. **God's Prompting: One way I feel God is prompting me to grow or change this week is:**
   "_____
   _____
   _____
   _____"

7. **Action Step: As a man of faith and leadership, one practical step I will take this week is:**
   "_____
   _____
   _____
   _____"

8. **Prayer Focus: I sense the need to bring this to God in prayer:**
   "_____
   _____
   _____
   _____"

9. *I also want to lift up these specific people or situations:*
   "_____
   _____
   _____
   _____"

10. **Brotherhood Check-in:**
    One truth I need to share or process with another man is:
    "_____
    _____
    _____
    _____"

11. I plan to connect with: _____ by (day/time): _____

12. **Refining at The Forge:**
    This week, God is shaping me most in the area of:
    "_____
    _____
    _____
    _____"

13. *I want to remain faithful in this process by:*
    "_____
    _____
    _____
    _____"

SECTION 5

Legacy in the Making: Inner Life & Endurance

(Weeks 31–40)

Every man leaves a legacy—but not every man leaves a godly one. This section is about cultivating the life that will outlive you. Here, the focus turns inward again, but this time with legacy in mind. Joy, gratitude, rest, reliability, and spiritual endurance—these aren't soft skills. They are the slow-burning coals that forge a man's impact over time.

As you press through these weeks, you'll reflect on how to stay the course, how to love deeply and laugh freely, how to defend truth without arrogance, and how to finish what you start. This isn't the sprint. It's the long obedience in the same direction.

Week 31
Building a Legacy of Faith

Intentionally living in a way that leaves a lasting impact on future generations.

A Legacy of Faith for Future Generations

George was a devoted father and grandfather, known for his unwavering faith and commitment to his family. Every Sunday, his house was filled with the laughter of his children and grandchildren, a testament to the close-knit bond they all shared. George often found himself reflecting on the legacy he wanted to leave behind—one that went beyond financial security or family traditions. He longed to leave a spiritual legacy that would carry his family through life's challenges long after he was gone.

One afternoon, as George sat on the porch reading his Bible, his grandson, Josiah, joined him with a question. "Grandpa, why do you always talk about God so much?" George smiled, sensing the opportunity he had been waiting for. He turned to Psalm 78:4 and read aloud, "We will not hide them from their children, but tell to the coming generation the glorious deeds of the Lord..." George explained that it was his responsibility—and his greatest joy—to share the stories of God's faithfulness with his family.

George shared his personal journey of faith with Josiah, recounting how God had been his anchor through both triumphs and trials. He spoke of the times when he had been laid off, when family members had fallen ill, and when life felt uncertain, yet God had always been faithful. George wanted Josiah to know that the same God who had guided him was there for his grandson, too.

Inspired by 2 Timothy 1:5, where Paul reflects on Timothy's sincere faith passed down from his grandmother Lois and mother Eunice, George decided to be even more intentional about building a legacy of faith. He began to organize monthly family devotion nights, where they would gather, read Scripture, pray, and share stories of God's work in their lives. It was a simple practice, but it brought the family closer, rooting them deeper in their shared faith.

One night, during one of these devotions, George watched as his daughter, Sarah, shared her own story of answered prayer, bringing tears to everyone's eyes. It was in that moment George realized his efforts were bearing fruit. The seeds of faith he had sown were growing in the hearts of his children and grandchildren, just as the faith of Timothy's grandmother had taken root in him.

George also made it a point to write letters to his grandchildren, sharing his favorite Bible verses, words of wisdom, and prayers for their futures. He wanted them to have a tangible reminder of his love and faith to hold onto, even when he was no longer with them. The letters became treasures, filled with heartfelt advice and testimonies of God's grace, passed down to be read and reread through the years.

As the years went by, George's family continued to honor the traditions he had started. His children and grandchildren grew to love those moments of shared faith, understanding that they were part of something bigger—a legacy that reached back to their grandfather and would extend far beyond them. They learned to value the importance of sharing their own faith stories, recognizing that each generation had a role in keeping the flame of belief alive.

George's life became a living testimony to Psalm 78:4 and 2 Timothy 1:5, showing how one man's commitment to God could ripple through generations. He didn't just tell his family about his faith; he showed them how to live it, day by day, with authenticity, love, and steadfast devotion.

In his final years, George was surrounded by the family he had nurtured in faith, his legacy shining brightly in each of their lives. He knew that he was leaving behind more than memories—he was leaving a foundation of faith that would carry them through anything.

Through his intentional efforts to share God's glorious deeds, George had built a legacy of faith that would outlast him, inspiring future generations to walk with God just as he had. His life was a powerful reminder that the most lasting impact we can make is not found in what we leave behind, but in who we help others become in Christ.

> Old Testament: Psalm 78:4 "We will not hide them from their children, but tell to the coming generation the glorious deeds of the Lord..."
>
> New Testament: 2 Timothy 1:5 "I am reminded of your sincere faith, a faith that dwelt first in your grandmother Lois and your mother Eunice..."

As Christian men, we are called to intentionally build a legacy of faith that will resonate through generations to come. Psalm 78:4 urges us to share "the glorious deeds of the Lord" with our children, ensuring that they understand the depth of God's love and faithfulness. This passing down of faith is echoed in 2 Timothy 1:5, where Paul acknowledges the sincere faith that first lived in Timothy's grandmother Lois and mother Eunice. Let us commit to living our lives in such a way that our faith becomes a living testimony, actively teaching and demonstrating God's truths to our families. By investing in their spiritual growth and modeling Christlike values, we can leave an indelible mark on future generations, guiding them to know and trust in the Lord we serve. In doing so, we fulfill our calling to be both faithful followers and devoted fathers, shaping a legacy that honors God and inspires those who come after us.

🛠 The Forge Weekly Reflection Sheet

Personal Study & Leadership Accountability Questions

1. Theme in My Life: This week's theme was
   "____"
   In my current life, I see this theme at work in the area of:
   "____
   ____"

2. Key Verse Insight: The Scripture that stood out most to me this week was:
   "____
   ____"

3. *Because it reminded/taught/convicted me that:*
   "____
   ____
   ____
   ____"

4. Connection—The story of __________ made me think about:
   "____
   ____"

5. *A similar situation in my life has been:*
   "____
   ____
   ____
   ____"

6. **God's Prompting:** One way I feel God is prompting me to grow or change this week is:
   "_____
   _____
   _____
   _____"

7. **Action Step:** As a man of faith and leadership, one practical step I will take this week is:
   "_____
   _____
   _____
   _____"

8. **Prayer Focus:** I sense the need to bring this to God in prayer:
   "_____
   _____
   _____
   _____"

9. *I also want to lift up these specific people or situations:*
   "_____
   _____
   _____
   _____"

10. **Brotherhood Check-in:**
    One truth I need to share or process with another man is:
    "_____
    _____
    _____
    _____"

11. I plan to connect with: _____ by (day/time): _____

12. Refining at The Forge:
    This week, God is shaping me most in the area of:
    "_____
    _____
    _____
    _____"

13. *I want to remain faithful in this process by:*
    "_____
    _____
    _____
    _____"

Week 32
The Role of Humor and Joy

Embracing joy and humor as tools for building relationships and diffusing tension.

The Power of Joy and Humor in Leadership

Tim was the manager of a bustling auto repair shop, a job that came with its fair share of stress, tight deadlines, and demanding customers. His team was a mix of seasoned mechanics and young apprentices, each with their own personalities and quirks. Lately, Tim had noticed that morale was low; the pressure to meet targets and the constant stream of problems had made the shop feel tense. The team was efficient, but the joy seemed to have drained out of the work.

One particularly hectic afternoon, Tim watched as one of his younger mechanics, Mike, struggled to fix a stubborn engine problem. Frustration was written all over his face, and the tension in the shop was palpable. Remembering Proverbs 17:22—"A joyful heart is good medicine, but a crushed spirit dries up the bones"—Tim knew that this was a moment where a little bit of humor could make a big difference.

Tim walked over, put on his best over-the-top announcer voice, and said, "Ladies and gentlemen, we're witnessing the world's greatest mechanic in action! Watch as Mike wrestles the beast of the engine bay! Will he triumph, or will the engine have the last word?" The whole shop burst into laughter, including Mike, who threw up his hands in mock defeat, grinning at the unexpected commentary.

Tim's lightheartedness broke the tension, and suddenly, the challenge didn't seem so overwhelming. Mike took a deep breath, calmed by the laughter, and returned to his work with renewed energy. Within minutes, the problem was fixed, and the entire team cheered him on, turning what had been a stressful moment into one of camaraderie and encouragement.

That small spark of humor changed the atmosphere in the shop. Tim realized that, just as Philippians 4:4 urged, he needed to "rejoice in the Lord always" and share that joy with his team, even in the middle of a busy workday. He began to intentionally incorporate more humor and positivity into his leadership, from sharing funny stories during lunch breaks to celebrating each small victory with light-hearted banter.

Tim's approach didn't just boost morale—it built stronger relationships among the team. The mechanics, who had once been just coworkers, started to feel more like a family. They began to look out for each other, share in each other's burdens, and approach challenges with a sense of unity rather than frustration.

One day, when the shop faced a particularly stressful deadline, Tim noticed the difference his intentional joy had made. The team worked tirelessly, but instead of being weighed down, they encouraged one another with jokes, shared laughter, and a sense of collective purpose. Tim's lighthearted spirit had created an environment where everyone felt valued and supported.

Even the customers noticed the change. One regular client, Mrs. Davis, commented, "I don't know what's going on here, but it's always a pleasure to come in—you all seem so happy!" Tim smiled, knowing that it was the joy of the Lord reflected in his team that made the difference.

Through his leadership, Tim learned that humor wasn't just about making people laugh; it was about creating a space where people felt safe, connected, and appreciated. By embracing joy and humor, he was able to diffuse tension, build trust, and foster a culture where everyone thrived.

Tim's commitment to leading with joy turned his shop into more than just a place of work—it became a place of refuge, where hard days were met with laughter and where every challenge was an opportunity to rejoice. He showed that even in the most routine or difficult moments, the joy of the Lord could shine through, lifting spirits and building bonds that were stronger than any stress they faced.

In embracing humor and joy, Tim not only became a better leader but also a light to everyone around him, reflecting God's love in the most practical and impactful ways. His shop was living proof that a joyful heart truly is good medicine, healing weary spirits and inspiring others to find joy in every circumstance.

> Old Testament: Proverbs 17:22 "A joyful heart is good medicine, but a crushed spirit dries up the bones."
>
> New Testament: Philippians 4:4 "Rejoice in the Lord always; again I will say, Rejoice."

As Christian men, we are encouraged to embrace joy and humor as vital tools for building relationships and diffusing tension in our lives. Proverbs 17:22 reminds us that "a joyful heart is good medicine," highlighting how laughter and positivity can uplift both ourselves and those around us, while a crushed spirit can bring about weariness. In Philippians 4:4, Paul urges us to "rejoice in the Lord always," emphasizing that our joy should be rooted in our relationship with Christ, regardless of our circumstances. By cultivating a spirit of joy and incorporating humor into our interactions, we create an environment where others feel welcomed and valued. Let us be men who reflect the joy of the Lord, using our laughter to strengthen bonds and lighten burdens, ultimately shining His light in a world that desperately needs it.

Men's Leadership Devotional

⚒ The Forge Weekly Reflection Sheet

Personal Study & Leadership Accountability Questions

1. **Theme in My Life: This week's theme was**
   "_____"
   In my current life, I see this theme at work in the area of:
   "_____
   _____"

2. **Key Verse Insight: The Scripture that stood out most to me this week was:**
   "_____
   _____"

3. *Because it reminded/taught/convicted me that:*
   "_____
   _____
   _____
   _____"

4. **Connection—The story of _____ made me think about:**
   "_____
   _____"

5. *A similar situation in my life has been:*
   "_____
   _____
   _____
   _____"

6. **God's Prompting:** One way I feel God is prompting me to grow or change this week is:
   "_____
   _____
   _____
   _____"

7. **Action Step:** As a man of faith and leadership, one practical step I will take this week is:
   "_____
   _____
   _____
   _____"

8. **Prayer Focus:** I sense the need to bring this to God in prayer:
   "_____
   _____
   _____
   _____"

9. *I also want to lift up these specific people or situations:*
   "_____
   _____
   _____
   _____"

10. **Brotherhood Check-in:**
    One truth I need to share or process with another man is:
    "_____
    _____
    _____
    _____"

11. I plan to connect with: _____ by (day/time): _____

12. **Refining at The Forge:**
    This week, God is shaping me most in the area of:
    "_____
    _____
    _____
    _____"

13. *I want to remain faithful in this process by:*
    "_____
    _____
    _____
    _____"

Week 33
Gratitude and Contentment

Cultivating an attitude of gratitude, leading with a sense of contentment in all circumstances.

Leading with Gratitude and Contentment

Frank was a dedicated family man, working hard to provide for his wife and two children. He ran a small landscaping business, which, while fulfilling, was often unpredictable. Some seasons brought plenty of work, while others were marked by slowdowns and tight budgets. Recently, the business had hit a rough patch, and Frank found himself struggling to make ends meet. As the bills piled up, his anxiety grew, and the weight of uncertainty pressed heavily on his shoulders.

One evening, after a long day of trying to drum up new clients with little success, Frank sat in his truck, feeling overwhelmed. He opened his Bible, searching for comfort, and his eyes landed on Psalm 107:1: "Oh give thanks to the Lord, for he is good, for his steadfast love endures forever!" It felt almost impossible to give thanks when he was so burdened, but Frank knew that gratitude was not about circumstances—it was about trusting in God's unchanging goodness.

Determined to shift his perspective, Frank began to list things he was thankful for: his loving family, his health, the loyal clients who had stuck with him, and the small blessings of each day. He remembered 1 Thessalonians

5:18, which instructed, "Give thanks in all circumstances; for this is the will of God in Christ Jesus for you." Frank realized that gratitude was a choice, and by embracing it, he could find contentment even in the most difficult times.

The next morning, Frank decided to lead his family in a new practice. Over breakfast, he invited everyone to share something they were grateful for, no matter how small. At first, it felt forced, especially with the stress hanging in the air, but soon it became a daily tradition that brought unexpected joy. His daughter, Lily, would share her gratitude for sunny days to play outside, while his son, Noah, expressed thanks for the fun of playing with the family dog.

One evening, as they sat around the table, Frank's wife, Maria, shared, "I'm thankful for the way we've been leaning on each other. Even when things are tough, I feel closer to all of you." Frank's heart swelled with a sense of peace that he hadn't felt in weeks. The financial challenges were still there, but his family was united, and their home was filled with a spirit of gratitude that overshadowed their worries.

As the months went on, Frank continued to cultivate this attitude of thankfulness, not just at home but also at work. He began expressing appreciation to his employees for their hard work, even when business was slow. He reached out to his clients, thanking them personally for their loyalty, and offered small, unexpected discounts as a gesture of his gratitude. This shift in focus changed the atmosphere of his business, and slowly but surely, new opportunities began to arise.

One day, Frank received a call from a large company that needed ongoing landscaping services for multiple properties. It was the break he had been praying for. As he hung up the phone, Frank took a moment to thank God—

not just for the new contract but for the lessons in gratitude and contentment that had carried him through the lean times.

Through it all, Frank learned that contentment wasn't about having everything go right but about trusting that God's provision was enough, whatever the circumstances. His gratitude turned what could have been a season of despair into one of growth and deepened faith.

Frank's commitment to gratitude became a guiding principle for his family and his business, reminding everyone around him that God's goodness is present in every situation. He showed that by focusing on the blessings rather than the burdens, we align our hearts with God's will and find joy that transcends our circumstances.

In choosing gratitude, Frank not only transformed his outlook but also inspired those around him to see life through the lens of God's steadfast love. His story became a powerful reminder that when we give thanks in all circumstances, we reflect Christ's light, bringing hope and contentment to a world that desperately needs both.

> Old Testament: Psalm 107:1 "Oh give thanks to the Lord, for he is good, for his steadfast love endures forever!"
>
> New Testament: 1 Thessalonians 5:18 "Give thanks in all circumstances; for this is the will of God in Christ Jesus for you."

As Christian men, cultivating an attitude of gratitude is essential for leading lives marked by contentment, regardless of our circumstances. Psalm 107:1 calls us to "give thanks to the Lord, for he is good; for his steadfast love endures forever," reminding us of the unchanging

274 The Forge

goodness of God, even in challenging times. In 1 Thessalonians 5:18, we are instructed to "give thanks in all circumstances; for this is the will of God in Christ Jesus for you." This powerful reminder encourages us to find reasons for gratitude, even amidst trials, as it aligns our hearts with God's perspective. By choosing to focus on His faithfulness and love, we foster a spirit of contentment that transforms our outlook on life. Let us commit to leading with gratitude, trusting that God's provisions are sufficient, and inspiring those around us to do the same. In this way, we reflect Christ's light and love to a world often marked by discontent.

Men's Leadership Devotional 275

✶ The Forge Weekly Reflection Sheet

Personal Study & Leadership Accountability Questions

1. **Theme in My Life: This week's theme was**
   " _____ "
   In my current life, I see this theme at work in the area of:
   " _____
   _____ "

2. **Key Verse Insight: The Scripture that stood out most to me this week was:**
   " _____
   _____ "

3. *Because it reminded/taught/convicted me that:*
   " _____
   _____
   _____
   _____ "

4. **Connection—The story of _____ made me think about:**
   " _____
   _____ "

5. *A similar situation in my life has been:*
   " _____
   _____
   _____
   _____ "

6. **God's Prompting: One way I feel God is prompting me to grow or change this week is:**
   "_____
   _____
   _____
   _____"

7. **Action Step: As a man of faith and leadership, one practical step I will take this week is:**
   "_____
   _____
   _____
   _____"

8. **Prayer Focus: I sense the need to bring this to God in prayer:**
   "_____
   _____
   _____
   _____"

9. *I also want to lift up these specific people or situations:*
   "_____
   _____
   _____
   _____"

10. **Brotherhood Check-in:**
    One truth I need to share or process with another man is:
    "_____
    _____
    _____
    _____"

11. I plan to connect with: _____ by (day/time): _____

12. **Refining at The Forge:**
    This week, God is shaping me most in the area of:
    "_____
    _____
    _____
    _____"

13. *I want to remain faithful in this process by:*
    "_____
    _____
    _____
    _____"

Week 34
Sabbath Rest

Understanding the importance of rest and renewal for effective leadership.

Embracing Sabbath Rest for Renewed Leadership

Edward was a driven man. As a business owner, father, and church elder, his schedule was always packed. He thrived on productivity, often working late into the night and squeezing in meetings between family commitments and church responsibilities. While Edward prided himself on his work ethic, the constant hustle was taking its toll. He was tired, irritable, and felt disconnected from God, his family, and even himself.

One Sunday morning, after another week of endless tasks, Edward sat in church feeling completely drained. As the pastor began to speak on the importance of rest, Edward' attention was drawn to Exodus 20:8-10: "Remember the Sabbath day, to keep it holy. Six days you shall labor, and do all your work..." The words hit him hard. He realized that, in his pursuit of success, he had neglected one of God's most basic commands—taking time to rest.

Later, the pastor read from Mark 2:27: "The Sabbath was made for man, not man for the Sabbath." Edward had always seen rest as a luxury, something he could squeeze in when everything else was done. But Jesus' words were clear: Sabbath was a gift, designed to refresh and renew, not a burden or an afterthought.

That afternoon, Edward sat down with his wife, Melissa, and confessed, "I've been running on empty. I think I've forgotten how to rest." Melissa nodded; she had seen the toll it was taking on him and their family. "We need to start honoring the Sabbath," she agreed. "Not just for ourselves, but as an example to our kids."

Determined to change, Edward decided to intentionally observe a weekly Sabbath. He set clear boundaries: no work emails, no to-do lists, and no stress about what wasn't getting done. Instead, he focused on reconnecting with God, spending quality time with his family, and simply being still. The first few weekends were challenging—he felt restless, anxious, and tempted to check his phone. But slowly, he began to embrace the quiet.

On one of these Sabbath days, Edward and his family took a walk in a nearby park. They laughed, played games, and shared a picnic. For the first time in a long time, Edward felt present—really present. As he watched his kids run and play, he felt his own spirit lifting, the weight of constant responsibility fading away.

Week after week, Edward found himself looking forward to the Sabbath. It became a time not just to rest his body, but to recharge his soul. He spent time reading Scripture, praying, and reflecting on God's goodness. He noticed that he was more patient, more attentive, and more at peace, both at home and in his leadership roles.

At work, Edward' renewed energy and clarity didn't go unnoticed. His employees saw a difference—he was more engaged, creative, and supportive. He even started encouraging his team to take their own rest seriously, modeling the importance of balance. The culture of the workplace began to shift as Edward' example showed that productivity was not about constant busyness but about working from a place of rest and renewal.

One Sunday, during a family devotion, Edward shared his journey with his kids. "I used to think that the more I did, the more valuable I was. But God showed me that rest is just as important as work. Sabbath is a gift—it's God's way of saying, 'I've got this, you don't have to do it all.'" His children listened intently, and Edward knew he was planting seeds of wisdom that would benefit them for a lifetime.

Through embracing the Sabbath, Edward learned that rest was not a sign of weakness but a source of strength. It allowed him to lead with a clear mind, a joyful heart, and a deep connection to God's purpose for his life. By honoring the rhythm of work and rest, he was able to lead more effectively, showing his family and those he guided that true leadership comes from a well-rested and God-centered life.

Edward' story became a powerful testimony of the importance of Sabbath rest. He discovered that when we take time to step back, recharge, and reconnect with God, we are better equipped to face the challenges ahead. His commitment to rest didn't just transform his leadership—it renewed his entire approach to life, showing that sometimes the most powerful thing we can do is simply to be still and know that He is God.

> Old Testament: Exodus 20:810 "Remember the Sabbath day, to keep it holy. Six days you shall labor, and do all your work..."
>
> New Testament: Mark 2:27 "And he said to them, 'The Sabbath was made for man, not man for the Sabbath.'"

As Christian men, understanding the significance of Sabbath rest is crucial for effective leadership and overall well-being. Exodus 20:8-10 reminds us to "remember the

Sabbath day, to keep it holy," highlighting that God Himself instituted a rhythm of rest amidst our labor. This divine principle allows us to recharge and reconnect with our Creator, ensuring we do not lead from a place of exhaustion. In Mark 2:27, Jesus clarifies, "The Sabbath was made for man, not man for the Sabbath," emphasizing that this day of rest is a gift meant to nurture our souls and refresh our spirits. By intentionally observing Sabbath rest, we model a balanced lifestyle for those we lead, demonstrating that renewal is essential for resilience and clarity in our responsibilities. Let us embrace this sacred time as a powerful means to deepen our relationship with God and empower our leadership, ensuring that we lead with wisdom and strength.

✖ The Forge Weekly Reflection Sheet

Personal Study & Leadership Accountability Questions

1. **Theme in My Life:** This week's theme was
   "_____"
   In my current life, I see this theme at work in the area of:
   "_____
   _____"

2. **Key Verse Insight:** The Scripture that stood out most to me this week was:
   "_____
   _____"

3. *Because it reminded/taught/convicted me that:*
   "_____
   _____
   _____
   _____"

4. **Connection—The story of _____ made me think about:**
   "_____
   _____"

5. *A similar situation in my life has been:*
   "_____
   _____
   _____
   _____"

6. **God's Prompting: One way I feel God is prompting me to grow or change this week is:**

   " _____

   _____

   _____

   _____ "

7. **Action Step: As a man of faith and leadership, one practical step I will take this week is:**

   " _____

   _____

   _____

   _____ "

8. **Prayer Focus: I sense the need to bring this to God in prayer:**

   " _____

   _____

   _____

   _____ "

9. *I also want to lift up these specific people or situations:*

   " _____

   _____

   _____

   _____ "

10. **Brotherhood Check-in:**
    One truth I need to share or process with another man is:

    " _____

    _____

    _____

    _____ "

11. I plan to connect with: _____ by (day/time): _____

12. Refining at The Forge:
    This week, God is shaping me most in the area of:
    "_____
    _____
    _____
    _____ "

13. *I want to remain faithful in this process by:*
    "_____
    _____
    _____
    _____ "

Week 35
Social Responsibility

Recognizing the call to address social issues and lead with compassion and justice.

Leading with Compassion and Justice

Jeffrey had always been involved in his church, serving in various ministries and attending small groups, but lately, something had been stirring in his heart. He couldn't ignore the social issues he saw around him—families in his city struggling with homelessness, underfunded schools, and a widening gap between the privileged and the disadvantaged. He had spent most of his life focused on his own community and immediate needs, but now, Jeffrey felt God calling him to do more.

One morning, during his quiet time, Jeffrey read Leviticus 19:18: "You shall love your neighbor as yourself…" The verse stuck with him, challenging him to think about what it truly meant to love his neighbor. Who was his neighbor? He thought of the story of the Good Samaritan in Luke 10, where Jesus asks, "Which of these three, do you think, proved to be a neighbor to the man who fell among the robbers?" The answer was clear: "The one who showed him mercy." Jeffrey realized that being a good neighbor went beyond offering help when it was convenient—it meant stepping into the messiness of other people's lives and showing mercy.

Later that week, Jeffrey attended a community meeting focused on addressing local homelessness. As he listened to city officials, nonprofit leaders, and advocates discuss the crisis, Jeffrey felt a strong conviction that this was where he was called to act. He had always thought of social issues as too big to solve, but now he knew that wasn't an excuse to stay on the sidelines. He could do something—he could show mercy to those in need.

The next day, Jeffrey reached out to a local shelter to volunteer. On his first day, he met a man named Carl, who had lost his job and home due to an injury and was struggling to get back on his feet. Instead of just serving Carl a meal, Jeffrey sat down to listen to his story. He realized that Carl wasn't just a statistic—he was a person with hopes, dreams, and dignity. Jeffrey felt his heart soften as he remembered Leviticus 19:18: love your neighbor as yourself.

Jeffrey began to volunteer regularly, not just at the shelter but also advocating for policy changes that would provide better support for those experiencing homelessness. He used his voice, resources, and influence to bring awareness to the issues plaguing his community, and he encouraged others from his church to join him in these efforts. His leadership became a catalyst for change, as more people began to see the importance of engaging with those on the margins.

One Saturday, Jeffrey organized a community cleanup event near a low-income housing area, where he had been building relationships with local families. While picking up trash alongside some of the residents, he met a single mother named Angela who had been struggling to find steady work. Jeffrey's compassion for her situation went beyond sympathy—he connected her with job training programs and even offered to help with childcare when she attended interviews.

In every interaction, Jeffrey reflected the heart of the Good Samaritan. He wasn't just helping people in passing; he was building relationships, advocating for justice, and treating each person with the love and respect they deserved. As his involvement deepened, Jeffrey realized that addressing social issues wasn't about solving every problem at once—it was about showing up, offering mercy, and making a tangible difference in someone's life.

Through his journey, Jeffrey discovered that true leadership wasn't just about serving within the walls of the church but also about stepping out into the world and meeting people where they were. By embracing his social responsibility, Jeffrey embodied the compassion and justice of Christ, living out the command to love his neighbor in a world that desperately needed it.

Jeffrey's story became a beacon of hope in his community, showing that one person's decision to love their neighbor could create ripples of change. His willingness to engage with social issues didn't just make a difference in the lives of those he served—it also inspired others to do the same, transforming his community with the mercy and love of Christ. Through his actions, Jeffrey reflected God's heart for humanity, proving that social responsibility and Christian leadership go hand in hand.

One morning, during his quiet time, Jeffrey read Leviticus 19:18: "You shall love your neighbor as yourself…" The verse stuck with him, challenging him to think about what it truly meant to love his neighbor. Who was his neighbor? He thought of the story of the Good Samaritan in Luke 10, where Jesus asks, "Which of these three, do you think, proved to be a neighbor to the man who fell among the robbers?" The answer was clear: "The one who showed him mercy." Jeffrey realized that being a good neighbor went beyond offering help when it was convenient—it meant stepping into the messiness of other people's lives and showing mercy.

Later that week, Jeffrey attended a community meeting focused on addressing local homelessness. As he listened to city officials, nonprofit leaders, and advocates discuss the crisis, Jeffrey felt a strong conviction that this was where he was called to act. He had always thought of social issues as too big to solve, but now he knew that wasn't an excuse to stay on the sidelines. He could do something—he could show mercy to those in need.

The next day, Jeffrey reached out to a local shelter to volunteer. On his first day, he met a man named Carl, who had lost his job and home due to an injury and was struggling to get back on his feet. Instead of just serving Carl a meal, Jeffrey sat down to listen to his story. He realized that Carl wasn't just a statistic—he was a person with hopes, dreams, and dignity. Jeffrey felt his heart soften as he remembered Leviticus 19:18: love your neighbor as yourself.

Jeffrey began to volunteer regularly, not just at the shelter but also advocating for policy changes that would provide better support for those experiencing homelessness. He used his voice, resources, and influence to bring awareness to the issues plaguing his community, and he encouraged others from his church to join him in these efforts. His leadership became a catalyst for change, as more people began to see the importance of engaging with those on the margins.

One Saturday, Jeffrey organized a community cleanup event near a low-income housing area, where he had been building relationships with local families. While picking up trash alongside some of the residents, he met a single mother named Angela who had been struggling to find steady work. Jeffrey's compassion for her situation went beyond sympathy—he connected her with job training programs and even offered to help with childcare when she attended interviews.

In every interaction, Jeffrey reflected the heart of the Good Samaritan. He wasn't just helping people in passing; he was building relationships, advocating for justice, and treating each person with the love and respect they deserved. As his involvement deepened, Jeffrey realized that addressing social issues wasn't about solving every problem at once—it was about showing up, offering mercy, and making a tangible difference in someone's life.

Through his journey, Jeffrey discovered that true leadership wasn't just about serving within the walls of the church but also about stepping out into the world and meeting people where they were. By embracing his social responsibility, Jeffrey embodied the compassion and justice of Christ, living out the command to love his neighbor in a world that desperately needed it.

Jeffrey's story became a beacon of hope in his community, showing that one person's decision to love their neighbor could create ripples of change. His willingness to engage with social issues didn't just make a difference in the lives of those he served—it also inspired others to do the same, transforming his community with the mercy and love of Christ. Through his actions, Jeffrey reflected God's heart for humanity, proving that social responsibility and Christian leadership go hand in hand.

Leading with Compassion and Social Responsibility

Ryan was a successful real estate developer, known in his city for transforming rundown neighborhoods into thriving communities. But as his career flourished, Ryan began to feel a tug on his heart. Every day, he passed by homeless camps and struggling families on his way to work, and it

292 The Forge

bothered him that these scenes were just steps away from his renovated buildings. He knew that his work was changing the landscape of the city, but he couldn't shake the feeling that he was missing something important.

One Sunday at church, Ryan listened intently as his pastor preached on Leviticus 19:18: "You shall not take vengeance or bear a grudge against the sons of your own people, but you shall love your neighbor as yourself..." The message was clear: loving your neighbor went beyond words; it required action. Ryan knew he was being called to do more than just build properties—he needed to build bridges of compassion.

Later that week, Ryan read the parable of the Good Samaritan in Luke 10:36-37, where Jesus asked, "Which of these three, do you think, proved to be a neighbor to the man who fell among the robbers?" The answer was obvious: "The one who showed him mercy." Ryan realized that true leadership wasn't just about success; it was about showing mercy and compassion to those often ignored by society.

Determined to make a difference, Ryan reached out to a local nonprofit that served the homeless and low-income families in the area. He met with the director, an energetic woman named Grace, who shared stories of people struggling to find affordable housing and the many obstacles they faced. Ryan felt moved by her passion and the harsh realities she described.

"Is there a way I can help?" Ryan asked, eager to get involved. Grace explained that they were working on a transitional housing project but were short on resources and facing challenges with city permits. Ryan knew this was his chance to use his skills and influence for a greater purpose.

Over the next few months, Ryan partnered with the nonprofit, using his expertise to navigate the permit process, connect with suppliers for discounted materials, and rally other local developers to contribute. He even set aside units in his new developments for affordable housing, ensuring that his projects didn't just beautify the city but also served those most in need.

One day, as Ryan visited the nearly completed transitional housing site, he met a young mother named Carla and her two children. They had been living in their car for months, and the new housing would give them a fresh start. "Thank you for what you're doing," Carla said, tears in her eyes. "You've given us hope."

Ryan's heart swelled with gratitude. He saw firsthand how his efforts were making a real difference, not just in the skyline of his city, but in the lives of people like Carla. He realized that addressing social issues wasn't just about charity; it was about justice and treating every person with the dignity they deserved.

Through his involvement, Ryan's perspective on leadership shifted. He began to see his work as a platform for change, where he could advocate for those who often went unheard. He spoke at community meetings, urging other business leaders to consider their social responsibility, and he shared his story in his church, encouraging others to find ways to show mercy in their own spheres of influence.

Ryan's commitment to addressing social issues with compassion and justice became a defining aspect of his leadership. He discovered that by stepping into the struggles of his community and actively loving his neighbors as himself, he was not just building properties—he was building a legacy of mercy and hope.

His journey served as a powerful reminder that the call to love and serve our neighbors goes beyond the familiar faces in our lives. It extends to the marginalized, the struggling, and the overlooked, inviting us to embody the love of Christ in tangible ways. Ryan's actions reflected the heart of the Good Samaritan, showing that when we lead with compassion and responsibility, we truly fulfill our calling as followers of Jesus.

> Old Testament: Leviticus 19:18 "You shall not take vengeance or bear a grudge against the sons of your own people, but you shall love your neighbor as yourself..."
>
> New Testament: Luke 10:3637 "Which of these three, do you think, proved to be a neighbor to the man who fell among the robbers? He said, 'The one who showed him mercy.'"

As Christian men, we are called to embrace our social responsibility by addressing pressing social issues with compassion and justice. Leviticus 19:18 commands us to "love your neighbor as yourself," highlighting the importance of treating others with dignity and respect, regardless of their circumstances. This foundational principle is echoed in Luke 10:36-37, where Jesus emphasizes that the true neighbor is the one who shows mercy. In a world often marked by division and indifference, we are invited to step into the shoes of those in need, advocating for justice and extending grace to those who are marginalized. Let us lead with a heart of compassion, actively engaging in the struggles of our communities and embodying the love of Christ through our actions. By doing so, we not only fulfill our calling as followers of Jesus but also make a tangible difference in the lives of others, reflecting God's heart for humanity.

⚒ The Forge Weekly Reflection Sheet

Personal Study & Leadership Accountability Questions

1. **Theme in My Life:** This week's theme was
   "_____"

   In my current life, I see this theme at work in the area of:
   "_____
   _____"

2. **Key Verse Insight:** The Scripture that stood out most to me this week was:
   "_____
   _____"

3. *Because it reminded/taught/convicted me that:*
   "_____
   _____
   _____"

4. **Connection**—The story of _____ made me think about:
   "_____
   _____"

5. *A similar situation in my life has been:*
   "_____
   _____
   _____"

6. **God's Prompting: One way I feel God is prompting me to grow or change this week is:**
   "_____
   _____
   _____
   _____"

7. **Action Step: As a man of faith and leadership, one practical step I will take this week is:**
   "_____
   _____
   _____
   _____"

8. **Prayer Focus: I sense the need to bring this to God in prayer:**
   "_____
   _____
   _____
   _____"

9. ***I also want to lift up these specific people or situations:***
   "_____
   _____
   _____
   _____"

10. **Brotherhood Check-in:**
    One truth I need to share or process with another man is:
    "_____
    _____
    _____
    _____"

11. I plan to connect with: _____ by (day/time): _____

12. Refining at The Forge:
    This week, God is shaping me most in the area of:
    "_____
    _____
    _____
    _____"

13. *I want to remain faithful in this process by:*
    "_____
    _____
    _____
    _____"

Week 36
Intentionality in Relationships

Building and maintaining intentional, meaningful relationships with others.

The Power of Intentional Friendship

Gary had always been the go-to guy for his friends—a dependable presence at church, reliable in his job, and a loving husband and father. But beneath his calm exterior, he often felt isolated, struggling silently with the weight of his responsibilities. His closest friend, Nick, noticed something was off. Instead of offering empty reassurances or avoiding the awkwardness, Nick chose to lean into their friendship with intentionality, reflecting Proverbs 27:6, "Faithful are the wounds of a friend."

One evening, Nick invited Gary to coffee. As they sat in the quiet corner of a local café, Nick gently asked, "How are you really doing, Gary?" Surprised by the direct question but sensing the sincerity behind it, Gary hesitated. Nick's eyes didn't waver. He listened intently, embodying Ephesians 4:2's call to bear with one another in love.

Gary opened up about his struggles—the stress at work, the strain in his marriage, and the feeling that he wasn't living up to the expectations he had set for himself. Nick didn't rush to fix things or offer quick advice. Instead, he offered his presence, encouraging Gary to lean on God's grace and to take one step at a time.

Over the weeks, Nick continued to check in, not as a task but as an act of love. He prayed with Gary, offered honest feedback when needed, and shared his own struggles, building a bridge of mutual vulnerability and trust. This intentional investment in their relationship wasn't always easy, but it was transformative. Nick's willingness to have hard conversations and be present reminded Gary of Christ's unwavering commitment to His people.

Through their friendship, Gary began to find strength, knowing he wasn't alone in his journey. Nick's intentionality became a lifeline, illustrating that when we invest time, honesty, and patience into our relationships, we create spaces where God's love can be experienced in tangible ways. The friendship didn't just impact Gary—it shaped both of them, drawing them closer to each other and to the heart of God.

> Old Testament: Proverbs 27:6 "Faithful are the wounds of a friend; profuse are the kisses of an enemy."
>
> New Testament: Ephesians 4:2 "With all humility and gentleness, with patience, bearing with one another in love..."

As Christian men, we are called to be intentional in building and maintaining meaningful relationships that reflect Christ's love and grace. Proverbs 27:6 reminds us that "faithful are the wounds of a friend," highlighting the value of honesty and accountability in true friendships, even when it involves difficult conversations. In Ephesians 4:2, we are urged to approach one another "with all humility and gentleness, with patience, bearing with one another in love." This call to intentionality requires us to invest time and effort into nurturing our relationships, creating a foundation of trust and support. By being present, listening actively, and encouraging one another, we foster a community that mirrors the heart of God. Let us strive to cultivate these deep connections, knowing that they not only enrich our lives but also empower us to be the hands and feet of Jesus in each other's journeys.

Men's Leadership Devotional 303

⚒ The Forge Weekly Reflection Sheet

Personal Study & Leadership Accountability Questions

1. **Theme in My Life: This week's theme was**
   "_____"

   In my current life, I see this theme at work in the area of:
   "_____
   _____"

2. **Key Verse Insight: The Scripture that stood out most to me this week was:**
   "_____
   _____"

3. *Because it reminded/taught/convicted me that:*
   "_____
   _____
   _____
   _____"

4. **Connection—The story of _____ made me think about:**
   "_____
   _____"

5. *A similar situation in my life has been:*
   "_____
   _____
   _____
   _____"

6. **God's Prompting:** One way I feel God is prompting me to grow or change this week is:

   "_____
   _____
   _____
   _____"

7. **Action Step:** As a man of faith and leadership, one practical step I will take this week is:

   "_____
   _____
   _____
   _____"

8. **Prayer Focus:** I sense the need to bring this to God in prayer:

   "_____
   _____
   _____
   _____"

9. *I also want to lift up these specific people or situations:*

   "_____
   _____
   _____
   _____"

10. **Brotherhood Check-in:**
    One truth I need to share or process with another man is:

    "_____
    _____
    _____
    _____"

11. I plan to connect with: _____ by (day/time): _____

12. **Refining at The Forge:**
    This week, God is shaping me most in the area of:
    "_____
    _____
    _____
    _____"

13. *I want to remain faithful in this process by:*
    "_____
    _____
    _____
    _____"

Week 37
Apologetics and Defense of Faith

Being equipped to articulate and defend one's faith in a thoughtful manner.

A Thoughtful Defense of Faith

Eric was known among his friends as the quiet, steady type—faithful to his church, devoted to his family, and committed to living out his beliefs in a genuine way. He often found himself in conversations about faith, but lately, these discussions had become more challenging. His coworker, Alan, a sharp and outspoken skeptic, frequently questioned the Christian worldview, challenging Eric's beliefs with probing questions that left him feeling unprepared.

One afternoon during lunch, Alan leaned across the table and asked, "Eric, how can you believe in a loving God with all the suffering in the world? And what about all those contradictions in the Bible? Doesn't that bother you?"

Eric hesitated, feeling a knot of anxiety in his chest. He knew the importance of 1 Peter 3:15: "But in your hearts honor Christ the Lord as holy, always being prepared to make a defense to anyone who asks you for a reason for the hope that is in you..." Yet, he realized he had not been ready to answer thoughtfully. Instead of dodging the question or responding defensively, Eric decided it was time to seek wisdom and equip himself to engage more confidently.

That evening, Eric turned to Proverbs 1:7: "The fear of the Lord is the beginning of knowledge; fools despise wisdom and instruction." He realized that defending his faith wasn't about winning arguments but about honoring God by seeking a deeper understanding. Eric dedicated time each day to study Scripture and read apologetic resources, learning how to address tough questions with clarity and compassion. He prayed for the right words and the humility to speak truth in love.

Over the next few weeks, Eric continued his journey of learning, attending a local apologetics seminar and engaging in conversations with other believers who had faced similar challenges. He practiced articulating his faith, focusing on how to explain the hope he had found in Christ in a way that was respectful and thoughtful.

One morning, as Eric and Alan were setting up for a presentation at work, Alan brought up their previous conversation. "I've been thinking about what we talked about, and honestly, I just don't get it. How can you be so confident in something that seems so… uncertain?"

Eric felt a calm confidence wash over him, the result of the preparation he had invested in. "I understand your doubts, Alan," he began, honoring Alan's perspective. "There was a time when I had a lot of questions too. But I found that faith isn't about having every answer—it's about trusting the character of God, even in the unknowns. The Bible isn't a list of contradictions; it's a cohesive story of redemption that addresses the human condition, something I've personally experienced."

Eric continued, carefully explaining how his faith provided hope amidst life's challenges, grounding his answers in

Scripture and evidence. He spoke of the historical reliability of the Bible, the resurrection of Christ, and how the message of the Gospel transformed his own life. Rather than shutting down the conversation, he invited Alan into a dialogue, encouraging him to explore these questions more deeply.

Alan listened, surprised by Eric's approach. Instead of feeling attacked, he felt respected, and his curiosity was piqued. "I never thought of it that way," Alan admitted. "Maybe I've been too quick to judge without really understanding."

Eric offered to share some of the resources that had helped him, and Alan agreed, appreciating Eric's humility and thoughtful engagement. It wasn't an instant conversion, but a seed was planted—one that could grow through continued conversations rooted in respect and truth.

Through this experience, Eric learned that being equipped to defend his faith was not about having all the answers but about being willing to listen, learn, and engage with grace. His readiness to articulate the hope within him became a powerful testimony, showing that faith and reason could coexist.

Eric's journey reminded him that true knowledge begins with reverence for God and a commitment to His truth. By honoring Christ as holy in his heart, Eric was able to engage in meaningful conversations that reflected the love and wisdom of God, shining a light in a world full of questions and doubts. His example inspired others to prepare themselves as defenders of the faith, encouraging a thoughtful, compassionate approach to sharing the Gospel.

The Forge

> Old Testament: Proverbs 1:7 "The fear of the Lord is the beginning of knowledge; fools despise wisdom and instruction."
>
> New Testament: 1 Peter 3:15 "But in your hearts honor Christ the Lord as holy, always being prepared to make a defense to anyone who asks you for a reason for the hope that is in you..."

As Christian men, we are called to be not just followers of Christ, but also articulate defenders of our faith. Proverbs 1:7 reminds us that true knowledge begins with a reverent fear of the Lord, urging us to seek wisdom and embrace instruction. This foundational humility empowers us to engage thoughtfully with those around us. In 1 Peter 3:15, we are instructed to always be prepared to share the hope that resides within us, honoring Christ in our hearts. Let us commit to deepening our understanding of Scripture and cultivating a spirit of readiness, so that we can confidently share our faith with grace and conviction, illuminating the truth of the Gospel in a world that desperately needs it.

Men's Leadership Devotional 311

✖ The Forge Weekly Reflection Sheet

Personal Study & Leadership Accountability Questions

1. **Theme in My Life: This week's theme was**
   " _____ "
   In my current life, I see this theme at work in the area of:
   " _____
   _____ "

2. **Key Verse Insight: The Scripture that stood out most to me this week was:**
   " _____
   _____ "

3. *Because it reminded/taught/convicted me that:*
   " _____
   _____
   _____
   _____ "

4. **Connection—The story of _____ made me think about:**
   " _____
   _____ "

5. *A similar situation in my life has been:*
   " _____
   _____
   _____ "

6. **God's Prompting: One way I feel God is prompting me to grow or change this week is:**
   "_____
   _____
   _____
   _____ "

7. **Action Step: As a man of faith and leadership, one practical step I will take this week is:**
   "_____
   _____
   _____
   _____ "

8. **Prayer Focus: I sense the need to bring this to God in prayer:**
   "_____
   _____
   _____
   _____ "

9. *I also want to lift up these specific people or situations:*
   "_____
   _____
   _____
   _____ "

10. **Brotherhood Check-in:**
    One truth I need to share or process with another man is:
    "_____
    _____
    _____
    _____ "

11. I plan to connect with: _____ by (day/time): _____

12. Refining at The Forge:
    This week, God is shaping me most in the area of:
    "_____
    _____
    _____
    _____"

13. *I want to remain faithful in this process by:*
    "_____
    _____
    _____
    _____"

Week 38
Building Trust and Reliability

Establishing trust through consistent actions and reliability in commitments.

The Power of Trust and Reliability

Stephen was a devoted husband, father, and manager at a local construction company. Known for his hardworking nature, Stephen prided himself on his work ethic. But at home, he often found himself overcommitted, juggling deadlines, meetings, and responsibilities. As a result, he frequently missed family dinners, his kids' games, and the promises he made to his wife, Rachel, to spend more quality time together. His intentions were good, but his actions often fell short, leaving his family feeling disappointed.

One evening, Stephen promised his son, Ethan, that he would be at his baseball game. "I'll be there, buddy. I wouldn't miss it for the world." Ethan's eyes lit up, excited to have his dad in the stands. But when a last-minute work issue came up, Stephen found himself caught between the demands of his job and his commitment to his son. Once again, work won out. By the time he arrived at the field, the game was over, and Ethan was sitting on the bench, head down.

The sting of letting his son down hit Stephen hard. Proverbs 25:19 came to mind: "Trust in a treacherous man in time of trouble is like a bad tooth or a foot that slips."

316 The Forge

Stephen realized that while he wasn't treacherous, his unreliability was eroding the trust his family had in him. He knew that if he wanted to be the kind of man his family could depend on, he needed to change.

Determined to rebuild trust, Stephen made a commitment to prioritize his family and honor his word. He began to set clearer boundaries at work, refusing to let last-minute tasks interfere with his commitments at home. Stephen also shared his struggles with his team, explaining that he needed to be more present for his family. To his surprise, they understood and supported him, even stepping up to help cover responsibilities when Stephen needed to be elsewhere.

Stephen's dedication to reliability extended beyond his family; he also wanted to be a consistent leader at work. He focused on being a man of his word, whether it was following through on promises to clients, showing up on time, or ensuring his crew had the resources they needed to succeed. Stephen knew that trust was built one small action at a time, and he was committed to being dependable in every area of his life.

One day, Stephen's boss called him into the office with an opportunity for a major project that would require careful management and oversight. "Stephen, I've watched how you've been stepping up lately. You've shown consistency and reliability, and I trust you to lead this project. I know you'll do a great job." Stephen felt a swell of gratitude, recalling Matthew 25:21: "Well done, good and faithful servant. You have been faithful over a little; I will set you over much." His small, consistent actions were paying off, not just in recognition but in opportunities that reflected his growing reputation as a trustworthy leader.

That evening, Stephen arrived home early, surprising Rachel and the kids with a homemade pizza night. As they laughed and shared stories around the table, Stephen felt the peace that comes from knowing he was living up to his commitments. He looked at Ethan and said, "I'm sorry for the times I've let you down, buddy. I'm going to do better, and I'm going to be there for you."

Ethan smiled, his trust in his dad slowly rebuilding. "Thanks, Dad. I know you will."

Through his journey, Stephen learned that reliability wasn't about never making mistakes; it was about consistently showing up and doing what he said he would do. By being faithful in the little things, he earned the trust of his family, his colleagues, and those around him. Stephen's commitment to being a dependable man not only strengthened his relationships but also reflected Christ's faithfulness in every aspect of his life.

Stephen's story became a testament to the power of trust and reliability. His willingness to prioritize his commitments, honor his word, and consistently follow through created a foundation of trust that transformed his leadership and his home. By embracing these values, Stephen showed that even the smallest acts of faithfulness could lead to great rewards, echoing the commendation of the master: "Well done, good and faithful servant."

> Old Testament: Proverbs 25:19 "Trust in a treacherous man in time of trouble is like a bad tooth or a foot that slips."
>
> New Testament: Matthew 25:21 "His master said to him, 'Well done, good and faithful servant. You have been faithful over a little; I will set you over much.'"

318 The Forge

As Christian men, building trust and reliability is essential for fostering strong, meaningful relationships and effective leadership. Proverbs 25:19 warns us that "trust in a treacherous man in time of trouble is like a bad tooth or a foot that slips," reminding us of the importance of integrity and consistency in our actions. We are called to be men of our word, embodying reliability in our commitments. In Matthew 25:21, we see the reward for faithfulness as the master commends the servant: "Well done, good and faithful servant." This illustrates that even small acts of faithfulness can lead to greater responsibilities and blessings. Let us strive to be dependable and trustworthy, ensuring that our friends, family, and colleagues know they can count on us. By consistently demonstrating our commitment through our actions, we reflect Christ's character and create a foundation of trust that strengthens our relationships and our witness in the world.

1. **Theme in My Life: This week's theme was**
   "_____"

   In my current life, I see this theme at work in the area of:
   "_____
   _____"

2. **Key Verse Insight: The Scripture that stood out most to me this week was:**
   "_____
   _____"

3. *Because it reminded/taught/convicted me that:*
   "_____
   _____
   _____
   _____"

4. **Connection—The story of _____ made me think about:**
   "_____
   _____"

5. *A similar situation in my life has been:*
   "_____
   _____
   _____
   _____"

6. **God's Prompting: One way I feel God is prompting me to grow or change this week is:**
   "_____
   _____
   _____
   _____"

7. **Action Step: As a man of faith and leadership, one practical step I will take this week is:**
   "_____
   _____
   _____
   _____ "

8. **Prayer Focus: I sense the need to bring this to God in prayer:**
   "_____
   _____
   _____
   _____ "

9. *I also want to lift up these specific people or situations:*
   "_____
   _____
   _____
   _____ "

10. **Brotherhood Check-in:**
    One truth I need to share or process with another man is:
    "_____
    _____
    _____
    _____ "

11. I plan to connect with: _____ by (day/time): _____

12. Refining at The Forge:
This week, God is shaping me most in the area of:

"_____
_____
_____
_____"

13. *I want to remain faithful in this process by:*

"_____
_____
_____
_____"

Week 39
Endurance in Trials

Demonstrating faith and perseverance during trials, inspiring others to trust God.

Faith and Endurance Through Trials

Jonathan was a respected community leader and father of three, known for his steadfast faith and calm demeanor. He was the kind of man people turned to for advice and encouragement, and he often led by example in his church. But when his business, a small family-owned hardware store, began to struggle due to a downturn in the economy, Jonathan found himself facing one of the toughest trials of his life. Sales plummeted, bills piled up, and the once-thriving business that he had built from the ground up was on the brink of collapse.

As the pressure mounted, Jonathan tried everything to keep the store afloat—working longer hours, cutting costs, and even dipping into his savings. But no matter what he did, it seemed like his efforts were not enough. The stress began to weigh on him, and doubts crept into his mind. One afternoon, after another disappointing day at the store, Jonathan sat alone in the back office, feeling utterly defeated.

He opened his Bible and found himself reading Job 23:10: "But he knows the way that I take; when he has tried me, I shall come out as gold." Jonathan was reminded that his current struggles were not the end of his story. Like Job, he was being refined, and this season of trial was an opportunity to grow stronger in his faith. He prayed, asking God for the strength to endure, even when the path ahead seemed uncertain.

Determined to trust God through the storm, Jonathan decided to share his struggles with his church community. One Sunday, he stood before the congregation and vulnerably opened up about his business challenges, admitting how hard it had been to remain hopeful. He quoted Hebrews 12:1, "Let us also lay aside every weight… and run with endurance the race that is set before us," and spoke about the importance of persevering through trials, not just for ourselves, but for those who are watching our journey.

As Jonathan spoke, he could see the faces of his family, friends, and community members, many of whom were also going through their own battles. He realized that his response to this trial wasn't just about his own growth—it was about inspiring others to keep their faith, even when life was hard. After the service, several people approached him, sharing their own stories of struggle and expressing gratitude for his honesty. Jonathan's openness had given them hope, reminding them that they were not alone in their battles.

In the weeks that followed, Jonathan continued to endure, holding on to the promise that God was with him every step of the way. His perseverance began to inspire others, not just within his church but also among his employees and customers, who saw him navigating hardship with grace and determination. Even when things looked bleak, Jonathan made it a point to encourage his staff, praying with them before opening each day and reminding them that their worth was not tied to the store's success, but to their identity in Christ.

Slowly, things began to turn around. A loyal customer referred Jonathan's store to a large contractor in need of supplies, bringing in a significant order that helped stabilize the business. While the challenges didn't disappear overnight, each small victory felt like a confirmation that God was honoring Jonathan's faith and endurance.

One evening, after closing up shop, Jonathan's eldest son, Luke, approached him. "Dad, I've seen how hard this has been for you, but you never gave up. Watching you trust God through all of this has made me want to do the same." Jonathan's eyes filled with tears. He realized that his endurance wasn't just shaping his own faith—it was leaving a lasting impact on his son and others around him.

Jonathan's journey through this trial taught him that endurance is not about having all the answers or always feeling strong—it's about trusting God's faithfulness, even in the darkest moments. By embracing his struggles with perseverance, Jonathan became a living testimony of Job 23:10 and Hebrews 12:1, demonstrating that when we run the race with endurance, we come out refined, strengthened, and equipped to inspire others.

His story reminded those around him that true strength is found not in avoiding hardship, but in facing it with faith, knowing that God is at work. Jonathan's perseverance lit the way for others to trust in God's promises, proving that every trial has the potential to shape us into something far greater than we could ever imagine.

> Old Testament: Job 23:10 "But he knows the way that I take; when he has tried me, I shall come out as gold."

326 The Forge

> New Testament: Hebrews 12:1 "Therefore, since we are surrounded by so great a cloud of witnesses, let us also lay aside every weight..."

As Christian men, demonstrating endurance in trials is a powerful testimony of our faith and perseverance. Job 23:10 reassures us that "when he has tried me, I shall come out as gold," reminding us that our struggles can refine us and strengthen our character, shaping us into the men God intends us to be. In Hebrews 12:1, we are encouraged to "lay aside every weight" and run with endurance the race set before us, surrounded by a "great cloud of witnesses." This imagery inspires us to remain steadfast, not only for our own growth but also to encourage others who are watching our journey. By trusting God through life's challenges, we can inspire those around us to lean on Him, demonstrating that true strength is found in reliance on Christ. Let us embrace our trials with faith, knowing that our perseverance can light the way for others to trust in God's faithfulness.

Men's Leadership Devotional 327

⚒ The Forge Weekly Reflection Sheet

Personal Study & Leadership Accountability Questions

1. **Theme in My Life: This week's theme was**
   "_____"
   In my current life, I see this theme at work in the area of:
   "_____
   _____"

2. **Key Verse Insight: The Scripture that stood out most to me this week was:**
   "_____
   _____"

3. ***Because it reminded/taught/convicted me that:***
   "_____
   _____
   _____"

4. **Connection—The story of _____ made me think about:**
   "_____
   _____"

5. ***A similar situation in my life has been:***
   "_____
   _____
   _____"

6. **God's Prompting: One way I feel God is prompting me to grow or change this week is:**

   "_____
   _____
   _____
   _____ "

7. **Action Step: As a man of faith and leadership, one practical step I will take this week is:**

   "_____
   _____
   _____
   _____ "

8. **Prayer Focus: I sense the need to bring this to God in prayer:**

   "_____
   _____
   _____
   _____ "

9. ***I also want to lift up these specific people or situations:***

   "_____
   _____
   _____
   _____ "

10. **Brotherhood Check-in:**
    One truth I need to share or process with another man is:

    "_____
    _____
    _____
    _____ "

11. I plan to connect with: _____ by (day/time): _____

12. Refining at The Forge:
    This week, God is shaping me most in the area of:
    "_____
    _____
    _____
    _____"

13. *I want to remain faithful in this process by:*
    "_____
    _____
    _____
    _____"

Week 40
Responding to Criticism

Handling criticism with grace and humility, using it for personal and spiritual growth.

Embracing Criticism with Grace and Humility

Paul was a well-respected leader in his church, known for his strong teaching and passion for ministry. He often led Bible studies and preached on Sundays, and many looked up to him as a role model. But beneath his confident exterior, Paul struggled with accepting criticism. He prided himself on doing things well and found it difficult when others pointed out areas where he could improve.

One Sunday, after delivering what he thought was a powerful sermon, Paul was approached by an older gentleman from the congregation, Mr. Thompson. Known for his candid nature, Mr. Thompson gently said, "Paul, I appreciated your message, but I felt like you focused more on your own stories than on the Scripture. Sometimes less of us and more of God's Word is what the people need."

Paul felt his face flush. His initial reaction was defensive. He had worked hard on that sermon, and hearing this critique felt like a blow. But as Mr. Thompson's words echoed in his mind, Paul remembered Proverbs 15:31: "The ear that listens to life giving reproof will dwell among the wise." He realized that this feedback wasn't meant to tear him down; it was an opportunity for growth.

332 The Forge

That evening, Paul prayed, asking God to help him handle criticism with humility and grace. He reflected on his own tendency to judge others, recalling Jesus' words in Luke 6:37: "Judge not, and you will not be judged; condemn not, and you will not be condemned..." Paul recognized that just as he was quick to offer feedback to others, he needed to be open to receiving it himself, without defensiveness.

Determined to grow from this experience, Paul decided to seek feedback intentionally. He reached out to Mr. Thompson, thanking him for his honesty and asking for more insights on how he could improve his preaching. Mr. Thompson was surprised but gladly agreed, offering to review Paul's outlines and provide constructive feedback.

Over the next few months, Paul embraced this new approach. He invited other trusted friends and colleagues to give him honest feedback on his sermons and leadership style. Each critique, though sometimes hard to hear, became a valuable lesson that sharpened his skills and deepened his understanding of how to better serve his congregation.

One day, after a particularly moving sermon that focused deeply on Scripture, a young man approached Paul. "Thank you for that message," he said. "It really spoke to me in a way I haven't felt before." Paul smiled, grateful not just for the compliment but for the journey that had brought him to that moment—the journey of listening, learning, and growing through criticism.

Through this process, Paul's preaching became more impactful, and his relationships within the church grew stronger. People saw a new humility in him—a willingness to learn and adapt that inspired others to be open to feedback in their own lives. Paul's openness to criticism became a powerful testimony of Proverbs 15:31 in action, showing that wisdom comes from a teachable spirit.

Paul's story didn't just end with personal growth; it set a tone within his church community. Others began to approach feedback with a spirit of grace, understanding that criticism, when received with humility, could lead to profound transformation. Paul often reminded his congregation, "God uses every voice, even the ones that challenge us, to shape us into who He wants us to be."

By embracing criticism, Paul learned to value the perspectives of those around him, recognizing that every piece of feedback was an opportunity to refine his character and ministry. His journey became a living example of how handling criticism with grace and humility can lead to personal and spiritual growth, inspiring others to do the same.

Paul's willingness to listen and learn, even when it was uncomfortable, reflected Christ's humility and set an example for his community. He demonstrated that true strength lies not in perfection but in a teachable heart that seeks wisdom from every experience, turning reproof into a pathway toward wisdom and grace.

> Old Testament: Proverbs 15:31 "The ear that listens to lifegiving reproof will dwell among the wise."
>
> New Testament: Luke 6:37 "Judge not, and you will not be judged; condemn not, and you will not be condemned..."

As Christian men, responding to criticism with grace and humility is vital for our personal and spiritual growth. Proverbs 15:31 teaches us that "the ear that listens to lifegiving reproof will dwell among the wise," reminding us that constructive criticism can lead to deeper

334 The Forge

understanding and wisdom if we approach it with an open heart. In Luke 6:37, Jesus cautions us not to judge or condemn others, encouraging a spirit of humility that allows us to reflect on our own shortcomings. When faced with criticism, let us strive to view it as an opportunity for growth rather than a personal attack. By embracing feedback with a teachable spirit, we can learn valuable lessons, strengthen our character, and model Christlike humility to those around us. In doing so, we not only grow closer to God but also inspire others to seek wisdom and grace in their own journeys.

⚒ The Forge Weekly Reflection Sheet

Personal Study & Leadership Accountability Questions

1. **Theme in My Life: This week's theme was**
   "_____"
   In my current life, I see this theme at work in the area of:
   "_____
   _____"

2. **Key Verse Insight: The Scripture that stood out most to me this week was:**
   "_____
   _____"

3. *Because it reminded/taught/convicted me that:*
   "_____
   _____
   _____
   _____"

4. **Connection—The story of _____ made me think about:**
   "_____
   _____"

5. *A similar situation in my life has been:*
   "_____
   _____
   _____
   _____"

6. **God's Prompting:** One way I feel God is prompting me to grow or change this week is:
   " _____
   _____
   _____ "

7. **Action Step:** As a man of faith and leadership, one practical step I will take this week is:
   " _____
   _____
   _____ "

8. **Prayer Focus:** I sense the need to bring this to God in prayer:
   " _____
   _____
   _____ "

9. *I also want to lift up these specific people or situations:*
   " _____
   _____
   _____ "

10. **Brotherhood Check-in:**
    One truth I need to share or process with another man is:
    " _____
    _____
    _____ "

11. I plan to connect with: _____ by (day/time): _____

12. **Refining at The Forge:**
    This week, God is shaping me most in the area of:
    "_____
    _____
    _____
    _____"

13. *I want to remain faithful in this process by:*
    "_____
    _____
    _____
    _____"

SECTION 6

Leading Together: Spiritual Influence and Faithfulness

(Weeks 41–52)

You weren't meant to lead alone. The final stretch of *The Forge* turns outward and upward—to the community of faith, the call to truth, and the legacy of faithful influence. These weeks will help you think about how to support your church, disciple your brothers, create emotionally safe spaces, and step into change with courage.

As we close the year, we return to the basics: small faithfulness, big vision, and the kind of leadership that reflects Christ in quiet, powerful ways. Whether you're mentoring others or still learning to find your voice, this is where you solidify the kind of man you're becoming—one shaped by God, walking in truth, and leading with love.

Week 41
Promoting Peace and Unity

Striving for peace and unity within the church and community, bridging divides.

Bridging Divides with Peace and Unity

Scott was a dedicated member of his church, involved in multiple ministries and well-loved by his congregation. But recently, he had noticed growing tensions among the church members. Different groups were forming, each with strong opinions about how things should be run—whether it was about worship styles, community outreach, or how to spend the church budget. What once felt like a unified body now seemed fractured, and Scott knew this division was hindering their mission.

One evening, after a particularly heated church meeting, Scott sat in the sanctuary, reflecting on Psalm 133:1: "Behold, how good and pleasant it is when brothers dwell in unity!" He longed for the days when the church felt like one family, working together for a common purpose. As he prayed, he was reminded that unity didn't just happen; it required effort, humility, and a willingness to listen.

Scott felt God prompting him to be a peacemaker. He turned to Ephesians 4:3: "Eager to maintain the unity of the Spirit in the bond of peace." Scott realized that promoting peace and unity was not about avoiding difficult conversations but about engaging with love and respect, actively working to bridge divides.

342 The Forge

Determined to make a difference, Scott began reaching out to different members of the church, inviting them to small gatherings where they could share their concerns and ideas in a more relaxed setting. He created a space for open dialogue, encouraging everyone to speak honestly while also listening to others. Scott emphasized the need to focus on their shared love for Christ and their common mission, rather than their differences.

During one of these gatherings, tensions flared between two ministry leaders with opposing views on how to run the youth program. Scott gently guided the conversation, reminding them of their mutual goal—to serve and support the young people in their church. "We're all on the same team," Scott said. "Let's find a way to combine our ideas and make this program even better."

His calm demeanor and commitment to understanding both sides began to break down walls. By seeking common ground and validating each person's perspective, Scott helped the group come up with a new approach that incorporated elements from both viewpoints. The leaders, who once felt like rivals, left the meeting feeling heard and appreciated, more willing to collaborate than before.

Scott's efforts extended beyond the church walls. He organized community events that brought people from different backgrounds together—potlucks, service projects, and even simple coffee mornings. These gatherings allowed the church to connect with their neighbors, fostering relationships that transcended social and cultural barriers. Through these acts, Scott showed that unity wasn't just about agreement but about respect, kindness, and a shared commitment to God's love.

One Sunday, the church held a special service dedicated to celebrating their unity in Christ. Different members were invited to share testimonies, including those who had previously been at odds. As they spoke, it became clear how far the church had come—how understanding and peacemaking had brought healing to their relationships.

As the service ended, Scott looked around and felt overwhelmed with gratitude. The church was not perfect, but it was moving in the right direction—toward unity and peace. He saw how his willingness to bridge divides, to promote dialogue, and to embrace differences had helped restore harmony.

Scott's journey taught him that promoting peace and unity was not about avoiding conflict but about approaching it with a heart committed to God's love. By striving to be a peacemaker, he had not only strengthened his church but had also created a ripple effect that reached into the wider community.

Scott's actions embodied the spirit of Psalm 133:1 and Ephesians 4:3, showing that when we are eager to maintain unity and peace, we reflect the true heart of Christ. His example inspired others to take up the mantle of peacemaking, ensuring that the church remained a beacon of hope, love, and togetherness in a divided world. Scott's story became a powerful reminder that unity is not just a goal—it's a journey worth pursuing, one conversation, one act of kindness, and one prayer at a time.

> Old Testament: Psalm 133:1 "Behold, how good and pleasant it is when brothers dwell in unity!"
>
> New Testament: Ephesians 4:3 "Eager to maintain the unity of the Spirit in the bond of peace."

344 The Forge

As Christian men, we are called to promote peace and unity both within the church and our communities, actively bridging divides that can separate us. Psalm 133:1 proclaims, "Behold, how good and pleasant it is when brothers dwell in unity!" This beautiful imagery invites us to recognize the joy that comes from harmonious relationships, reflecting God's love to the world. In Ephesians 4:3, we are urged to be "eager to maintain the unity of the Spirit in the bond of peace," reminding us that unity is not just a passive state but an active pursuit. Let us commit ourselves to being peacemakers, seeking to understand different perspectives and finding common ground with those around us. By fostering an atmosphere of respect and collaboration, we can create a vibrant community that honors God and demonstrates the power of His love in overcoming division. In doing so, we fulfill our role as ambassadors of Christ, embodying the peace He calls us to share.

⚒ The Forge Weekly Reflection Sheet

Personal Study & Leadership Accountability Questions

1. **Theme in My Life: This week's theme was**
   "_____"

   In my current life, I see this theme at work in the area of:
   "_____
   _____"

2. **Key Verse Insight: The Scripture that stood out most to me this week was:**
   "_____
   _____"

3. ***Because it reminded/taught/convicted me that:***
   "_____
   _____
   _____
   _____"

4. **Connection—The story of _____ made me think about:**
   "_____
   _____"

5. ***A similar situation in my life has been:***
   "_____
   _____
   _____
   _____"

6. **God's Prompting:** One way I feel God is prompting me to grow or change this week is:

   " _____
   _____
   _____
   _____ "

7. **Action Step:** As a man of faith and leadership, one practical step I will take this week is:

   " _____
   _____
   _____
   _____ "

8. **Prayer Focus:** I sense the need to bring this to God in prayer:

   " _____
   _____
   _____
   _____ "

9. *I also want to lift up these specific people or situations:*

   " _____
   _____
   _____
   _____ "

10. **Brotherhood Check-in:**
    One truth I need to share or process with another man is:

    " _____
    _____
    _____
    _____ "

11. I plan to connect with: _____ by (day/time): _____

12. **Refining at The Forge:**
    This week, God is shaping me most in the area of:
    "_____
    _____
    _____
    _____"

13. *I want to remain faithful in this process by:*
    "_____
    _____
    _____
    _____"

Week 42
Advocating for the Truth

Upholding and advocating for biblical truth in a culture of relativism.

Upholding Truth in a Culture of Relativism

Justin was a high school history teacher who was deeply committed to his faith. He loved his job and enjoyed inspiring his students to think critically about the world around them. However, in recent years, Justin had noticed a growing trend in his classroom—a reluctance to accept any absolute truths. His students often embraced the idea that everyone's opinion was equally valid, even when it contradicted objective facts. It was a mindset that left Justin concerned, especially when it came to discussions that touched on morality and faith.

One afternoon, during a discussion about historical figures who stood for their beliefs, a student named Madison raised her hand. "Mr. Thompson, isn't it true that what's right for one person might not be right for another? I mean, everyone should just follow their own truth, right?"

Justin knew this was a teachable moment, not just about history but about the deeper principles that shaped his own life. He remembered Psalm 119:160: "The sum of your word is truth, and every one of your righteous rules endures forever." Justin understood that God's truth was not just one of many opinions—it was the solid foundation that stood the test of time.

350 The Forge

With compassion and respect, Justin addressed Madison's question. "I understand why it might seem that way, especially today when we hear a lot about living your truth. But I believe there's a difference between personal perspectives and absolute truths. The Bible teaches us that truth is not just subjective—it's anchored in God's Word, which endures forever."

He continued, "Jesus said in John 8:32, 'And you will know the truth, and the truth will set you free.' The truth He's talking about is liberating because it gives us a clear direction and purpose, not just based on feelings or changing opinions, but on something solid and unchanging."

The room grew quiet as Justin spoke, and he could see that his words were resonating with some of the students. They weren't used to hearing someone talk about truth with such conviction, especially in a culture that often avoided definitive statements. Justin wasn't trying to force his beliefs on anyone, but he wanted his students to consider that some truths—like those found in Scripture—offered a freedom that subjective beliefs could never provide.

After class, a few students approached Justin, curious to know more about what he had shared. One student, Alex, admitted, "I've always thought truth was just whatever you want it to be, but now I'm starting to wonder if there's more to it. How can you be so sure?"

Justin smiled, grateful for the opportunity to delve deeper. "It's not always easy, and I've had my own questions along the way. But the more I study God's Word, the more I see how it aligns with reality and how it offers a consistent, unchanging guide for life. It's not just about believing something because it feels right—it's about discovering a truth that's bigger than us, one that truly sets us free."

Justin offered to share resources and invited Alex to ask questions anytime. He didn't have all the answers, but he was willing to walk alongside his students as they explored these big ideas.

Through his willingness to speak truth with grace, Justin became a trusted voice in his students' lives, not just as a teacher but as a mentor who valued the pursuit of wisdom. His classroom became a place where open dialogue about faith, truth, and morality was welcomed, providing a counter-narrative to the relativism that often pervaded their world.

Justin's commitment to advocating for biblical truth made an impact that extended far beyond the classroom. He showed his students that while opinions may vary, some truths are steadfast, offering a reliable compass in a sea of uncertainty. By standing firm in his convictions and sharing the truth with humility, Justin became a beacon of hope, guiding others toward the freedom that only Christ's truth can provide.

His example reminded his students—and himself—that in a world full of shifting beliefs, God's Word remains a rock of enduring truth. Through his quiet courage, Justin illustrated that advocating for biblical truth is not about winning arguments but about inviting others to experience the transformative power of knowing and embracing what is eternally true.

> Old Testament: Psalm 119:160 "The sum of your word is truth, and every one of your righteous rules endures forever."
>
> New Testament: John 8:32 "And you will know the truth, and the truth will set you free."

352 The Forge

As Christian men, we are called to advocate for biblical truth in a world often swayed by relativism and uncertainty. Psalm 119:160 affirms, "The sum of your word is truth, and every one of your righteous rules endures forever," reminding us that God's truth is timeless and unchanging, providing a solid foundation for our lives. In John 8:32, Jesus proclaims, "And you will know the truth, and the truth will set you free," highlighting the liberating power of embracing and sharing His Word. In a culture that may challenge our beliefs, let us stand firm in our convictions, grounding ourselves in Scripture and seeking to understand its implications for our lives and the world around us. By living out and advocating for the truth, we not only strengthen our own faith but also become beacons of hope for others, guiding them toward the freedom that comes from knowing Christ. Let us boldly share this truth, embodying the love and grace that flows from it, as we navigate a complex world together.

Men's Leadership Devotional

✖ The Forge Weekly Reflection Sheet

Personal Study & Leadership Accountability Questions

1. **Theme in My Life: This week's theme was**
   "_____"

   In my current life, I see this theme at work in the area of:
   "_____
   _____"

2. **Key Verse Insight: The Scripture that stood out most to me this week was:**
   "_____
   _____"

3. *Because it reminded/taught/convicted me that:*
   "_____
   _____
   _____
   _____"

4. **Connection—The story of _____ made me think about:**
   "_____
   _____"

5. *A similar situation in my life has been:*
   "_____
   _____
   _____
   _____"

6. **God's Prompting:** One way I feel God is prompting me to grow or change this week is:

   "_____
   _____
   _____
   _____"

7. **Action Step:** As a man of faith and leadership, one practical step I will take this week is:

   "_____
   _____
   _____
   _____"

8. **Prayer Focus:** I sense the need to bring this to God in prayer:

   "_____
   _____
   _____
   _____"

9. *I also want to lift up these specific people or situations:*

   "_____
   _____
   _____
   _____"

10. **Brotherhood Check-in:**
    One truth I need to share or process with another man is:

    "_____
    _____
    _____
    _____"

11. I plan to connect with: _____ by (day/time): _____

12. Refining at The Forge:
    This week, God is shaping me most in the area of:
    "_____
    _____
    _____
    _____"

13. *I want to remain faithful in this process by:*
    "_____
    _____
    _____
    _____"

Week 43
Utilizing Spiritual Gifts

Recognizing and using personal spiritual gifts for the benefit of the church and community.

Discovering the Power of Spiritual Gifts

Brandon had always been a man of quiet faith, dedicated to his family and church, but he never thought of himself as someone particularly gifted. He admired those who preached with conviction, led worship with passion, or organized community outreaches with ease. He often felt his contributions were small, almost invisible, but he was faithful in the tasks he knew—showing up early to set up chairs, staying late to clean up, and quietly supporting behind the scenes.

One Sunday, the pastor announced that the church needed someone to help with an upcoming building project. The budget was tight, and the church couldn't afford professional help. Brandon, who worked as a carpenter, hesitated at first but felt a nudge in his spirit. He remembered the words from Exodus 31:3, where God spoke of filling people with ability, intelligence, and craftsmanship. Could it be that his skills weren't just for his job but for God's work too?

He approached the pastor after the service and offered his help. Brandon began to work on the project, bringing his expertise and creativity to the renovation. As he measured, cut, and built, he realized he wasn't just fixing

358 The Forge

walls and building structures—he was contributing something deeply valuable to his church family. The work became an act of worship, a way to pour out the skills God had given him.

During the weeks that followed, others began to notice Brandon's dedication. Inspired by his quiet leadership, several men from the church volunteered to assist, eager to learn from his craftsmanship. Brandon, now more aware of his own spiritual gifts, started mentoring these men, teaching them skills while sharing the gospel through his actions. He began to understand 1 Peter 4:10's call to be good stewards of God's varied grace, using his gift to serve others.

Through this simple act of service, Brandon's role in the church transformed. What began as a construction project blossomed into a ministry of encouragement and discipleship. Brandon's willingness to use his gifts inspired others to step forward, recognizing that everyone, regardless of their talent, has something valuable to contribute.

The church building was completed, but the true impact was seen in the community of men who had grown closer, both to God and to each other, through shared work and service. Brandon's story became a powerful reminder that when we embrace our spiritual gifts, no matter how ordinary they seem, we become vessels of God's grace, building His kingdom in ways we never imagined.

> Old Testament: Exodus 31:3 "And I have filled him with the Spirit of God, with ability and intelligence, with knowledge and all craftsmanship..."
>
> New Testament: 1 Peter 4:10 "As each has received a gift, use it to serve one another, as good stewards of God's varied grace."

As Christian men, recognizing and utilizing our spiritual gifts is essential for the health and growth of both the church and our communities. In Exodus 31:3, we see how God fills individuals with His Spirit, granting them "ability and intelligence, with knowledge and all craftsmanship" to fulfill His purposes. This illustrates that our gifts are divinely appointed and meant for significant contributions to the Body of Christ. Similarly, 1 Peter 4:10 encourages us to "use it to serve one another, as good stewards of God's varied grace," reminding us that our gifts are not for our own benefit but for the edification of others. Let us embrace our unique talents and passions, seeking ways to serve and uplift those around us. By doing so, we honor God's grace and create a vibrant community that reflects His love and purpose, inspiring others to discover and share their own gifts as essential parts of God's design for a thriving, unified Body of Christ.

⚒ The Forge Weekly Reflection Sheet

Personal Study & Leadership Accountability Questions

1. **Theme in My Life:** This week's theme was
   "_____"
   In my current life, I see this theme at work in the area of:
   "_____
   _____"

2. **Key Verse Insight: The Scripture that stood out most to me this week was:**
   "_____
   _____"

3. *Because it reminded/taught/convicted me that:*
   "_____
   _____
   _____
   _____"

4. **Connection—The story of _____ made me think about:**
   "_____
   _____"

5. *A similar situation in my life has been:*
   "_____
   _____
   _____
   _____"

6. **God's Prompting:** One way I feel God is prompting me to grow or change this week is:
   " _____
   _____
   _____
   _____ "

7. **Action Step:** As a man of faith and leadership, one practical step I will take this week is:
   " _____
   _____
   _____
   _____ "

8. **Prayer Focus:** I sense the need to bring this to God in prayer:
   " _____
   _____
   _____
   _____ "

9. *I also want to lift up these specific people or situations:*
   " _____
   _____
   _____
   _____ "

10. **Brotherhood Check-in:**
    One truth I need to share or process with another man is:
    " _____
    _____
    _____
    _____ "

11. I plan to connect with: _____ by (day/time): _____

12. Refining at The Forge:
This week, God is shaping me most in the area of:
"_____
_____
_____
_____"

13. *I want to remain faithful in this process by:*
"_____
_____
_____
_____"

Week 44
Healthy Boundaries

Establishing and respecting boundaries in relationships, promoting personal and spiritual health.

The Power of Healthy Boundaries

Jason was a devoted husband, father, and leader in his church. Known for his kind heart and willingness to help, he was the go-to person whenever anyone had a problem. From assisting with house repairs to offering late-night counsel, Jason was always there, ready to lend a hand. However, his constant availability came at a cost. He often found himself stretched thin, exhausted, and neglecting his own family's needs in the process.

One afternoon, Jason received a call from his friend, Tom, who was going through a tough time. Tom had been leaning heavily on Jason for advice and support, calling almost daily. While Jason genuinely wanted to help, he was beginning to feel overwhelmed by Tom's constant requests. That day, as Jason listened to Tom's latest issue, he realized that his own emotional reserves were running low. He hung up the phone, feeling more drained than ever, and recognized that something needed to change.

Jason thought of Proverbs 25:17: "Let your foot be seldom in your neighbor's house, lest he have his fill of you and hate you." The verse reminded him that even well-intentioned support can become burdensome if boundaries are not respected. Jason didn't resent Tom, but he knew that if he didn't establish some limits, their friendship—and his own well-being—would suffer.

Jason also reflected on Galatians 6:5: "For each will have to bear his own load." He realized that constantly stepping in to solve Tom's problems was not only exhausting for him but was also preventing Tom from taking responsibility for his own struggles. Jason prayed for wisdom, asking God to help him find a way to set boundaries that would honor both his needs and his friendship with Tom.

The next time Tom called, Jason decided to approach the conversation differently. After listening to Tom's concerns, he gently said, "Tom, I've been happy to support you, but I've noticed that I've been doing a lot of the heavy lifting lately. I think it might be helpful for both of us if we each take some responsibility for our own loads. I'm here for you, but I also need to make sure I'm taking care of my own family and responsibilities."

Tom was initially taken aback, but Jason's honest and respectful approach opened the door for a deeper conversation. They talked about finding a balance—how Jason could still be supportive without becoming overburdened, and how Tom could seek other resources and begin taking more ownership of his own challenges. Jason even offered to help Tom connect with a support group that could provide additional guidance and encouragement.

To Jason's surprise, setting boundaries didn't damage their friendship—it strengthened it. Tom respected Jason's honesty and began to lean less on Jason alone, seeking out other support systems. Jason, on the other hand, felt a renewed sense of balance, allowing him to be more present with his own family and focus on his personal responsibilities.

As Jason established healthier boundaries, he noticed a positive shift in all his relationships. He became more intentional about carving out time for rest, prayer, and quality moments with his wife and children. He learned that saying no was not a failure to help—it was a necessary step toward maintaining his own spiritual and emotional health.

By respecting his own limits and encouraging others to do the same, Jason modeled the importance of boundaries within his church community. He led workshops on healthy boundaries, sharing his experiences and emphasizing that setting limits was not about pushing people away but about creating space for mutual respect and growth.

Jason's journey showed those around him that boundaries are not barriers—they are bridges that allow for healthier, more balanced relationships. By following the wisdom of Proverbs 25:17 and Galatians 6:5, he demonstrated that it's possible to be supportive without losing oneself in the process. His example encouraged others to communicate openly, respect one another's needs, and build connections that were both strong and sustainable.

Through his willingness to establish and uphold boundaries, Jason found a new rhythm of life—one that honored God, respected his commitments, and allowed him to serve others without sacrificing his own well-being. His story became a testament to the power of boundaries, showing that when we respect our limits and those of others, we create relationships that reflect Christ's love, grace, and wisdom.

> Old Testament: Proverbs 25:17 "Let your foot be seldom in your neighbor's house, lest he have his fill of you and hate you."

368 The Forge

> New Testament: Galatians 6:5 "For each will have to bear his own load."

As Christian men, establishing and respecting healthy boundaries in our relationships is vital for promoting both personal and spiritual health. Proverbs 25:17 advises, "Let your foot be seldom in your neighbor's house," reminding us that maintaining appropriate boundaries prevents over-dependence and fosters mutual respect. In Galatians 6:5, we are instructed, "For each will have to bear his own load," emphasizing the importance of personal responsibility in our interactions. By recognizing our limits and the limits of others, we create space for genuine connections that are free from resentment and burnout. Healthy boundaries enable us to support one another without losing sight of our own needs and callings. Let us strive to communicate openly, ensuring that our relationships are built on respect and understanding, ultimately leading to deeper connections that reflect Christ's love and grace.

🛠 The Forge Weekly Reflection Sheet

Personal Study & Leadership Accountability Questions

1. **Theme in My Life: This week's theme was**
   "____"
   In my current life, I see this theme at work in the area of:
   "____
   ____"

2. **Key Verse Insight: The Scripture that stood out most to me this week was:**
   "____
   ____"

3. ***Because it reminded/taught/convicted me that:***
   "____
   ____
   ____
   ____"

4. **Connection—The story of _________ made me think about:**
   "____
   ____"

5. ***A similar situation in my life has been:***
   "____
   ____
   ____
   ____"

6. **God's Prompting:** One way I feel God is prompting me to grow or change this week is:

   " _____
   _____
   _____
   _____ "

7. **Action Step:** As a man of faith and leadership, one practical step I will take this week is:

   " _____
   _____
   _____
   _____ "

8. **Prayer Focus:** I sense the need to bring this to God in prayer:

   " _____
   _____
   _____
   _____ "

9. *I also want to lift up these specific people or situations:*

   " _____
   _____
   _____
   _____ "

10. **Brotherhood Check-in:**
    One truth I need to share or process with another man is:

    " _____
    _____
    _____
    _____ "

11. I plan to connect with: _____ by (day/time): _____

12. Refining at The Forge:
    This week, God is shaping me most in the area of:
    "_____
    _____
    _____
    _____"

13. *I want to remain faithful in this process by:*
    "_____
    _____
    _____
    _____"

Week 45
Living a Life of Worship

Viewing all aspects of life as an act of worship, glorifying God in daily activities.

Worship in the Everyday

Samuel was a devoted Christian, deeply involved in his church's worship team and known for his heartfelt guitar playing during Sunday services. He loved those moments on stage, where he felt closest to God, lost in the music that glorified His name. But during the week, Samuel often found himself feeling disconnected from that sense of worship. Between the demands of his job as a sales manager, household chores, and caring for his young kids, worship seemed confined to Sunday mornings, leaving the rest of his week feeling routine and ordinary.

One day, Samuel read Psalm 29:2: "Ascribe to the Lord the glory due his name; worship the Lord in the splendor of holiness." He felt convicted, realizing that he was reserving his worship for a few select moments rather than seeing all of his life as an opportunity to honor God. The verse reminded him that God's glory was not confined to the walls of the church—it was present in every aspect of his daily life.

Eager to shift his mindset, Samuel turned to Romans 12:1: "I appeal to you therefore, brothers, by the mercies of God, to present your bodies as a living sacrifice..." He realized that living a life of worship meant viewing everything he did as a way to glorify God, from his interactions at work to the way he treated his family.

The next morning, Samuel began his day with a prayer, asking God to help him see his everyday tasks as acts of worship. At work, he approached his meetings with a renewed sense of purpose, seeing his role not just as a job but as a chance to reflect God's integrity and kindness. He treated his colleagues with respect, listened with patience, and went out of his way to encourage those who were struggling, seeing these small actions as ways to honor God.

Later that evening, Samuel found himself washing the dishes after dinner, a task he usually rushed through without much thought. As he scrubbed, he began to thank God for the simple blessings in his life—a loving family, the food on their table, and the home they shared. He realized that even in these quiet, mundane moments, he could worship by expressing gratitude and taking joy in the everyday provisions of God's grace.

Samuel's new perspective also transformed how he interacted with his children. Instead of seeing their bedtime routine as a chore, he began to see it as an opportunity to demonstrate God's love. He read Bible stories with enthusiasm, prayed with his kids before they went to sleep, and used their nightly conversations to teach them about God's goodness in their lives.

One evening, as Samuel was tucking his daughter into bed, she looked up at him and said, "Daddy, I love when you sing to us before bed. It makes me feel happy." Samuel smiled, realizing that his acts of worship were impacting his family in profound ways, creating an atmosphere of love and peace that extended far beyond Sunday services.

Samuel's newfound approach to worship began to ripple out into every area of his life. His coworkers noticed his positive attitude, his wife appreciated his attentiveness at home, and his children felt his love in the little moments. Samuel realized that worship was not confined to the songs he played on his guitar but was woven into the fabric of his everyday actions, thoughts, and words.

His journey showed him that when we present our lives as living sacrifices, as Romans 12:1 encourages, we invite God into every moment, turning the ordinary into the extraordinary. By choosing to glorify God in all he did, Samuel found a deeper connection to his faith, one that went beyond music and into the heart of his daily life.

Samuel's life became a testimony to the truth that worship is not just an event—it's a lifestyle. By embracing this mindset, he not only honored God but also inspired those around him to see their own daily routines as opportunities for worship. Samuel's story was a powerful reminder that every task, no matter how small, can be an act of devotion when done with a heart that seeks to glorify God. His life of worship became a beacon of God's love, demonstrating that every moment is an opportunity to ascribe glory to the Lord, just as Psalm 29:2 calls us to do.

> Old Testament: Psalm 29:2 "Ascribe to the Lord the glory due his name; worship the Lord in the splendor of holiness."
>
> New Testament: Romans 12:1 "I appeal to you therefore, brothers, by the mercies of God, to present your bodies as a living sacrifice..."

As Christian men, we are called to live a life of worship that extends beyond Sunday services and permeates every aspect of our daily activities. Psalm 29:2 reminds us to "ascribe to the Lord the glory due his name; worship the

376 The Forge

Lord in the splendor of holiness," inviting us to recognize God's majesty in our everyday lives. Romans 12:1 reinforces this call by urging us to "present your bodies as a living sacrifice," highlighting that our acts—whether work, family interactions, or personal pursuits—can be expressions of worship. When we approach each day with the intention of glorifying God, even mundane tasks become opportunities to honor Him and reflect His character. Let us embrace this mindset, viewing every moment as a chance to demonstrate our love for God and serve others, thereby turning our lives into a continuous act of worship that points others to His grace and goodness.

🛠 The Forge Weekly Reflection Sheet

Personal Study & Leadership Accountability Questions

1. **Theme in My Life: This week's theme was**
   "____"
   In my current life, I see this theme at work in the area of:
   "____
   ____"

2. **Key Verse Insight: The Scripture that stood out most to me this week was:**
   "____
   ____"

3. ***Because it reminded/taught/convicted me that:***
   "____
   ____
   ____
   ____"

4. **Connection—The story of _________ made me think about:**
   "____
   ____"

5. ***A similar situation in my life has been:***
   "____
   ____
   ____
   ____"

6. **God's Prompting:** One way I feel God is prompting me to grow or change this week is:

   "_____
   _____
   _____
   _____"

7. **Action Step:** As a man of faith and leadership, one practical step I will take this week is:

   "_____
   _____
   _____
   _____"

8. **Prayer Focus:** I sense the need to bring this to God in prayer:

   "_____
   _____
   _____
   _____"

9. *I also want to lift up these specific people or situations:*

   "_____
   _____
   _____
   _____"

10. **Brotherhood Check-in:**
    One truth I need to share or process with another man is:

    "_____
    _____
    _____
    _____"

11. I plan to connect with: _____ by (day/time): _____

12. Refining at The Forge:
    This week, God is shaping me most in the area of:
    "_____
    _____
    _____
    _____"

13. *I want to remain faithful in this process by:*
    "_____
    _____
    _____
    _____"

Week 46
Supporting Church Leadership

Actively supporting and encouraging church leaders, fostering a healthy church environment.

Supporting Church Leadership with Encouragement and Wisdom

Greg was a dedicated member of his church, known for his steady involvement in various ministries. He loved his church family and was passionate about seeing the congregation grow. But recently, he sensed a heaviness in the church leadership. The pastor, Pastor Walt, was tirelessly working to navigate a season of change—new programs, financial challenges, and the shifting needs of the congregation were stretching him thin. Greg noticed that Pastor Walt often looked weary, and the burden of leading seemed to weigh heavily on his shoulders.

One evening, during a Bible study, Greg read 1 Chronicles 12:32: "Of Issachar, men who had understanding of the times, to know what Israel ought to do..." Greg felt convicted. The men of Issachar were celebrated not only for their wisdom but for their ability to support their leaders with timely and thoughtful guidance. Greg realized that supporting his pastor didn't just mean attending church services—it meant actively engaging in the needs of the church and its leadership.

382 The Forge

Greg decided to start by reaching out. After Sunday service, he approached Pastor Walt and asked if they could grab coffee. During their meeting, Greg didn't offer advice or critique. Instead, he simply listened as Pastor Walt shared his heart—the joys and the struggles, the wins and the weariness. Greg could sense how much Pastor Walt cared for the church, but he also saw how overwhelmed he was by the weight of his responsibilities.

Remembering Hebrews 13:17—"Obey your leaders and submit to them, for they are keeping watch over your souls"—Greg recognized the immense spiritual responsibility Pastor Walt carried. He knew that supporting his pastor meant more than just words; it required action. Greg thanked Pastor Walt for his leadership, assuring him that his hard work didn't go unnoticed. "You're doing a great job, Pastor. And we're here to help shoulder the load with you."

Greg then rallied a group of church members to form a support team for Pastor Walt and the church staff. They organized prayer meetings specifically for the leadership, interceding for wisdom, strength, and guidance. Greg also coordinated practical support, like setting up volunteer teams to assist with church events, freeing up the leaders to focus on their primary responsibilities.

One evening, during a church leadership meeting, Greg and his team presented a small token of appreciation—a framed verse of Hebrews 13:17 with a note that read, "We see you. We thank you. And we stand with you." Pastor Walt was moved, visibly touched by the outpouring of support. The simple gesture reminded him that he wasn't alone in his calling; his congregation was actively behind him, praying and working alongside him.

As the weeks passed, the church began to feel more energized. Pastor Walt, encouraged by the tangible support, found renewed strength in his ministry. The congregation also felt the difference; as the leaders were uplifted, the entire church environment became more vibrant and collaborative. Members began taking ownership of various roles, lightening the load on the leadership and fostering a sense of shared purpose.

Greg's commitment to supporting his church leaders went beyond organizing teams; he made it a point to personally check in with Pastor Walt regularly, offering a listening ear, words of encouragement, and even the occasional practical help, like setting up the sanctuary or running errands. He realized that sometimes the most powerful way to support a leader was simply to show up consistently and faithfully.

Through these actions, Greg became an embodiment of the wisdom of the men of Issachar and the exhortation of Hebrews 13:17. He demonstrated that supporting church leadership is not a passive role but an active commitment to uplift those who guide the spiritual journey of the congregation.

Greg's efforts helped foster a healthier church environment, where leaders felt valued, and members felt empowered to contribute. His story served as a reminder that when we actively support our leaders, we not only honor their calling but also strengthen the entire church body, creating a community that works together to glorify God.

By understanding the challenges and opportunities faced by church leaders and offering support with humility and respect, Greg showed that everyone has a role in fostering a vibrant, God-centered church. His actions inspired others to get involved, turning the church into a true partnership of leaders and members, united in their mission to advance God's kingdom.

> Old Testament: 1 Chronicles 12:32 "Of Issachar, men who had understanding of the times, to know what Israel ought to do..."
>
> New Testament: Hebrews 13:17 "Obey your leaders and submit to them, for they are keeping watch over your souls..."

As Christian men, actively supporting and encouraging our church leaders is vital for fostering a healthy and vibrant church environment. In 1 Chronicles 12:32, we read about the men of Issachar, who possessed "understanding of the times" and knew how to guide Israel effectively. This wisdom reminds us of the importance of recognizing the challenges and opportunities our leaders face, equipping us to offer our support and insight. In Hebrews 13:17, we are called to "obey your leaders and submit to them, for they are keeping watch over your souls," highlighting the spiritual responsibility our leaders carry. By uplifting our church leaders through prayer, encouragement, and active participation, we contribute to a culture of respect and collaboration. Let us commit to standing beside them, ensuring they feel supported in their calling, and working together to build a community that glorifies God and advances His kingdom.

Men's Leadership Devotional

⚒ The Forge Weekly Reflection Sheet

Personal Study & Leadership Accountability Questions

1. **Theme in My Life:** This week's theme was
   " _____ "
   In my current life, I see this theme at work in the area of:
   " _____
   _____ "

2. **Key Verse Insight:** The Scripture that stood out most to me this week was:
   " _____
   _____ "

3. *Because it reminded/taught/convicted me that:*
   " _____
   _____
   _____ "

4. **Connection**—The story of _____ made me think about:
   " _____
   _____ "

5. *A similar situation in my life has been:*
   " _____
   _____
   _____ "

6. **God's Prompting: One way I feel God is prompting me to grow or change this week is:**
   "_____
   _____
   _____
   _____"

7. **Action Step: As a man of faith and leadership, one practical step I will take this week is:**
   "_____
   _____
   _____
   _____"

8. **Prayer Focus: I sense the need to bring this to God in prayer:**
   "_____
   _____
   _____
   _____"

9. *I also want to lift up these specific people or situations:*
   "_____
   _____
   _____
   _____"

10. **Brotherhood Check-in:**
    One truth I need to share or process with another man is:
    "_____
    _____
    _____
    _____"

11. I plan to connect with: _____ by (day/time): _____

12. **Refining at The Forge:**
    This week, God is shaping me most in the area of:
    "_____
    _____
    _____
    _____"

13. *I want to remain faithful in this process by:*
    "_____
    _____
    _____
    _____"

Week 47
Long term Vision

Developing a long-term vision for personal life, family, and community service.

Crafting a Vision for the Future

Raymond was a successful business owner, a loving husband, and a dedicated father of three. Though his life appeared full and productive, Raymond often felt a lingering sense of restlessness. His days were packed with meetings, family obligations, and church commitments, but deep down, he knew he was drifting through life without a clear direction. One evening, as he sat quietly after another hectic day, Raymond stumbled upon Proverbs 29:18: "Where there is no prophetic vision the people cast off restraint, but blessed is he who keeps the law."

Raymond realized that, while he was busy, he lacked a clear vision for his personal life, his family, and his impact on the community. His efforts were scattered, driven by immediate needs rather than a purposeful long-term goal. He knew that without a vision, he was simply reacting to life rather than shaping it.

Determined to change, Raymond spent time in prayer, seeking God's guidance for his future. He also turned to Philippians 3:14: "I press on toward the goal for the prize of the upward call of God in Christ Jesus." This verse resonated deeply, reminding him that his life wasn't just about daily achievements but about pursuing a higher calling. Raymond knew he needed a clear, God-centered vision that would guide his actions and keep him focused on what truly mattered.

Raymond began by crafting a personal vision statement. He envisioned a life where he was not just successful in business but also intentional about his spiritual growth, a loving leader in his home, and an active contributor to his community. He wrote down goals for each area: deepening his relationship with God, investing quality time with his wife and children, and using his resources and skills to support community initiatives that aligned with his values.

He then shared this vision with his family. Over a Saturday breakfast, Raymond gathered his wife, Lisa, and their kids around the table. "I've been thinking a lot about where we're going as a family," he said. "I want us to be more than just busy. I want us to have a purpose, a vision that guides our choices." He shared his goals and invited them to contribute their own ideas, creating a family vision that included faith, service, and meaningful time together.

Together, they decided to set aside one evening a week for family devotions and community service projects. They started small, volunteering at a local food pantry, but the impact was immediate. The kids were excited to be involved, and the time spent serving together brought them closer as a family. Raymond saw the difference a clear vision was making—not just in his own life but in his family's dynamics and their sense of purpose.

Raymond also applied his long-term vision to his business, using it as a platform for community outreach. He began mentoring young entrepreneurs, offering internships to local high school students, and setting aside a portion of his profits to support local charities. His employees were inspired by his leadership, and the business became known not just for its success but for its positive impact on the community.

As the months passed, Raymond noticed a profound shift. His days were still busy, but they were filled with intentional actions that aligned with his vision. He was pressing on, not aimlessly, but toward a clearly defined goal that honored God and impacted those around him. He found joy in knowing that his efforts were part of a bigger picture, and his family shared in that excitement.

One evening, Raymond's son, Nathan, approached him. "Dad, I really liked helping at the food pantry. Can we do more stuff like that?" Raymond smiled, knowing that his vision was planting seeds of service and purpose in his children's hearts. He was not just living a life of impact; he was creating a legacy that would inspire his family for generations to come.

Raymond's story became a powerful example in his church and community. He often shared how developing a long-term vision had transformed his approach to life, helping him to stay focused and committed even when challenges arose. His testimony encouraged others to seek God's guidance in crafting their own visions, reminding them that a life without purpose is a life without direction.

Through his journey, Raymond demonstrated that a compelling vision is not just about personal ambition but about aligning one's life with God's will. By pressing on toward the goal, he was able to inspire his family and community to join him in a shared pursuit of faith, service, and impact. Raymond's life became a testament to the power of vision, showing that when we seek God's guidance and keep our eyes on the ultimate prize, we can build a legacy that honors Him and touches the world.

392 The Forge

>Old Testament: Proverbs 29:18 "Where there is no prophetic vision the people cast off restraint, but blessed is he who keeps the law."
>
>New Testament: Philippians 3:14 "I press on toward the goal for the prize of the upward call of God in Christ Jesus."

As Christian men, developing a long-term vision for our personal lives, families, and community service is essential for purposeful living. Proverbs 29:18 reminds us that "where there is no prophetic vision the people cast off restraint," emphasizing the need for clear direction and goals to guide our actions. A compelling vision helps us stay focused and committed, ensuring that we live intentionally and with purpose. In Philippians 3:14, Paul encourages us to "press on toward the goal for the prize of the upward call of God in Christ Jesus," inspiring us to keep our eyes on the ultimate reward while actively pursuing our God-given aspirations. By prayerfully crafting a vision that aligns with God's will, we can inspire our families and communities to join us in this journey, creating a legacy of faith, service, and impact that extends far beyond our immediate circumstances. Let us commit to seeking God's guidance as we establish and pursue our long-term vision, trusting that He will direct our paths and empower us to fulfill our calling.

⚒ The Forge Weekly Reflection Sheet

Personal Study & Leadership Accountability Questions

1. **Theme in My Life: This week's theme was**
   "_____"
   In my current life, I see this theme at work in the area of:
   "_____
   _____"

2. **Key Verse Insight: The Scripture that stood out most to me this week was:**
   "_____
   _____"

3. *Because it reminded/taught/convicted me that:*
   "_____
   _____
   _____
   _____"

4. **Connection—The story of _____ made me think about:**
   "_____
   _____"

5. *A similar situation in my life has been:*
   "_____
   _____
   _____
   _____"

6. **God's Prompting: One way I feel God is prompting me to grow or change this week is:**
   " _____
   _____
   _____
   _____ "

7. **Action Step: As a man of faith and leadership, one practical step I will take this week is:**
   " _____
   _____
   _____
   _____ "

8. **Prayer Focus: I sense the need to bring this to God in prayer:**
   " _____
   _____
   _____
   _____ "

9. *I also want to lift up these specific people or situations:*
   " _____
   _____
   _____
   _____ "

10. **Brotherhood Check-in:**
    One truth I need to share or process with another man is:
    " _____
    _____
    _____
    _____ "

11. I plan to connect with: _____ by (day/time): _____

12. **Refining at The Forge:**
    This week, God is shaping me most in the area of:
    "_____
    _____
    _____
    _____"

13. *I want to remain faithful in this process by:*
    "_____
    _____
    _____
    _____"

Week 48
Empathy and Compassion

Practicing empathy, seeking to understand others' experiences and feelings.

Leading with Empathy and Compassion

Jack was a hardworking manager at a manufacturing plant, known for his dedication and no-nonsense approach. He prided himself on efficiency and results, often focusing on the task at hand rather than the people behind it. But lately, morale among his team had been low, and productivity was slipping. Complaints about burnout, stress, and a lack of support were becoming more frequent, and Jack couldn't understand why. He was meeting deadlines and hitting targets—wasn't that what mattered most?

One afternoon, Jack noticed one of his employees, Marcus, sitting alone in the break room, staring blankly at his lunch. Jack usually avoided getting too personal with his team, but something about Marcus's demeanor prompted him to sit down. As they talked, Marcus shared that he was struggling to balance work and his personal life—his wife was ill, and his son was having trouble at school. Marcus admitted that the pressures of the job were becoming overwhelming, and he felt like he was failing everywhere.

Jack was taken aback. He had always seen Marcus as a reliable worker, but he hadn't considered the challenges

Marcus faced outside of work. Jack thought of Zechariah 7:9: "Render true judgments, show kindness and mercy to one another..." He realized that he had been focused solely on the job, missing the opportunity to show empathy and support to those who worked alongside him every day.

Feeling convicted, Jack remembered Colossians 3:12: "Put on then, as God's chosen ones, holy and beloved, compassionate hearts..." Jack knew that as a leader, his role wasn't just about managing tasks—it was about understanding and supporting his team. He apologized to Marcus for not noticing his struggles sooner and assured him that he wasn't alone. They spent the next hour talking, not about work, but about life, family, and the challenges Marcus was facing.

Inspired by their conversation, Jack decided it was time to change his approach. He began to make empathy and compassion a priority in his leadership, taking time to check in with his team members, not just about their work but about their well-being. He held regular team meetings where he encouraged open communication, allowing everyone to share their concerns without fear of judgment. Jack also implemented small changes to make the work environment more supportive, like offering flexible hours and mental health resources.

As Jack practiced empathy, he saw a noticeable shift in his team. Productivity improved, but more importantly, the atmosphere became one of mutual respect and care. His employees felt heard, valued, and understood, and they were more willing to go the extra mile because they knew their leader genuinely cared about them.

One day, during a team meeting, Jack opened up about his own struggles, sharing how he had often let the pressures of work overshadow his ability to connect with others. He admitted that he was learning the importance of empathy and compassion, and he thanked his team for their patience and honesty. The room was quiet, and then one by one, his team members expressed their gratitude for Jack's willingness to change. They appreciated his efforts to listen and create a more compassionate workplace.

Through this journey, Jack learned that practicing empathy wasn't a sign of weakness—it was a powerful way to lead. By putting on a compassionate heart, as Colossians 3:12 called him to do, Jack became not just a manager but a true leader who inspired his team to work together with understanding and kindness.

Jack's transformation showed his team that leadership was about more than just meeting goals; it was about seeing people as individuals with their own stories, struggles, and needs. His willingness to show kindness and mercy, as Zechariah 7:9 urged, fostered a culture where everyone felt valued and supported, and where success was measured not just in numbers but in the strength of their relationships.

Jack's story became a reminder to everyone that empathy and compassion are not optional—they are essential elements of true leadership. By actively listening, seeking to understand, and allowing his heart to be moved by the needs of others, Jack embodied the love of Christ in his workplace, transforming his team and becoming an instrument of God's grace in a world that desperately needs it.

> Old Testament: Zechariah 7:9 "Thus says the Lord of hosts, Render true judgments, show kindness and mercy to one another..."

400 The Forge

> New Testament: Colossians 3:12 "Put on then, as God's chosen ones, holy and beloved, compassionate hearts..."

As Christian men, practicing empathy and compassion is vital in our interactions with others, allowing us to genuinely understand and connect with their experiences and feelings. Zechariah 7:9 calls us to "render true judgments, show kindness and mercy to one another," reminding us that God desires us to treat others with love and fairness, reflecting His character in our relationships. In Colossians 3:12, we are encouraged to "put on then, as God's chosen ones, holy and beloved, compassionate hearts," emphasizing that empathy is not just an option but a calling for those who follow Christ. By actively listening and seeking to understand the struggles and joys of those around us, we cultivate an environment of support and love. Let us commit to being men of compassion, allowing our hearts to be moved by the needs of others, and thereby becoming instruments of God's grace in a world that longs for understanding and kindness.

Men's Leadership Devotional 401

1. **Theme in My Life: This week's theme was**
   "_____"

   In my current life, I see this theme at work in the area of:
   "_____
   _____"

2. **Key Verse Insight: The Scripture that stood out most to me this week was:**
   "_____
   _____"

3. ***Because it reminded/taught/convicted me that:***
   "_____
   _____
   _____
   _____"

4. **Connection—The story of _____ made me think about:**
   "_____
   _____"

5. ***A similar situation in my life has been:***
   "_____
   _____
   _____
   _____"

6. **God's Prompting: One way I feel God is prompting me to grow or change this week is:**
   "_____
   _____
   _____
   _____"

7. **Action Step: As a man of faith and leadership, one practical step I will take this week is:**
   "_____
   _____
   _____
   _____"

8. **Prayer Focus: I sense the need to bring this to God in prayer:**
   "_____
   _____
   _____
   _____"

9. *I also want to lift up these specific people or situations:*
   "_____
   _____
   _____
   _____"

10. **Brotherhood Check-in:**
    One truth I need to share or process with another man is:
    "_____
    _____
    _____
    _____"

11. I plan to connect with: _____ by (day/time): _____

12. Refining at The Forge:
This week, God is shaping me most in the area of:

"_____
_____
_____
_____"

13. *I want to remain faithful in this process by:*

"_____
_____
_____
_____"

Week 49
Promoting Lifelong Learning

Committing to continuous growth and learning in faith, leadership, and personal development.

Embracing Lifelong Learning for Growth and Leadership

Tyler was a respected leader in his church and community. A successful business owner and devoted family man, he had always prided himself on his ability to handle challenges and provide guidance. But as he approached his late 50s, Tyler began to feel that he was coasting on what he already knew rather than actively growing. He often found himself giving the same advice, leading in the same ways, and feeling increasingly disconnected from the newer members of his team and church.

One morning, during his quiet time, Tyler read Proverbs 18:15: "An intelligent heart acquires knowledge, and the ear of the wise seeks knowledge." It struck him that he hadn't been seeking new knowledge or pushing himself to learn as he once had. Instead, he had settled into a comfortable routine, relying on past experiences rather than seeking fresh insights. Tyler realized that if he wanted to be an effective leader and follower of Christ, he needed to embrace lifelong learning once again.

He also reflected on 2 Peter 3:18: "But grow in the grace and knowledge of our Lord and Savior Jesus Christ." Tyler understood that his spiritual growth was not meant to plateau but to continue deepening throughout his life. The verse reminded him that knowing Christ was a journey, not a destination, and that growth in grace and knowledge was essential to becoming the man God called him to be.

Determined to reignite his passion for learning, Tyler made a plan. He enrolled in an online theology course to deepen his understanding of Scripture, and he began reading books on leadership, faith, and personal development. He also sought out a mentor—an older, wise gentleman from his church named Jack, who had spent decades in ministry. Tyler admired Jack's humility and insight and knew he could learn much from his wisdom.

Tyler also became intentional about listening more and talking less, especially in meetings and conversations. He started asking questions of his younger colleagues, eager to understand their perspectives and learn from their experiences. This approach not only expanded Tyler's knowledge but also built bridges between generations in his workplace and church, fostering a culture of mutual respect and collaboration.

One evening, Tyler attended a community seminar led by a speaker who was twenty years his junior. Initially, Tyler hesitated, thinking he already knew the basics of the topic—community engagement. But the young speaker's fresh ideas and enthusiasm challenged Tyler's thinking and inspired him to try new approaches. Tyler realized that learning from those younger or with different experiences wasn't a sign of weakness—it was a sign of wisdom.

As Tyler continued to pursue learning, his approach to leadership transformed. He started incorporating new strategies into his business, which led to improved team morale and innovative problem-solving. At church, he shared his journey of growth with his men's group, encouraging them to embrace learning in all its forms—

through Scripture, relationships, and the challenges of everyday life.

One Sunday, during a discussion with his group, Tyler shared how his commitment to lifelong learning was changing him. "I used to think that because I was older, I had all the answers," he admitted. "But God has shown me that there is always more to learn, more to understand, and more ways to grow. When we stop learning, we stop living the full life God has for us."

Tyler's humility and dedication to growth inspired those around him. Younger men in the group felt encouraged to seek mentorship, and older men were reminded that their journey of learning was far from over. Tyler's example became a living testament to the wisdom of Proverbs 18:15 and 2 Peter 3:18, showing that continuous learning is not just about acquiring knowledge but about growing closer to God and becoming more effective in every area of life.

Through his renewed commitment to learning, Tyler enriched his own faith, revitalized his leadership, and created a ripple effect of growth within his community. He demonstrated that no matter our age or stage in life, there is always more to learn, more ways to serve, and more opportunities to deepen our relationship with Christ.

Tyler's story became a powerful reminder that lifelong learning is a gift—a way to keep our hearts and minds open to God's ongoing work in our lives. By embracing this mindset, Tyler not only transformed himself but also inspired others to pursue the abundant life that comes from never ceasing to learn and grow in the knowledge and grace of our Lord.

408 The Forge

> Old Testament: Proverbs 18:15 "An intelligent heart acquires knowledge, and the ear of the wise seeks knowledge."
>
> New Testament: 2 Peter 3:18 "But grow in the grace and knowledge of our Lord and Savior Jesus Christ..."

As Christian men, promoting lifelong learning is essential for our growth in faith, leadership, and personal development. Proverbs 18:15 teaches us that "an intelligent heart acquires knowledge," encouraging us to be proactive in seeking wisdom and understanding throughout our lives. This pursuit of knowledge is vital for equipping us to lead effectively and to serve others with insight and compassion. In 2 Peter 3:18, we are urged to "grow in the grace and knowledge of our Lord and Savior Jesus Christ," highlighting that our spiritual journey is one of continual progress and deepening relationship with God. Let us commit ourselves to ongoing learning—whether through prayer, study, mentorship, or experience—so that we may become more effective disciples and leaders in our families, communities, and churches. By embracing a mindset of growth, we not only enrich our own lives but also inspire those around us to pursue the abundant life that comes from knowing Christ more deeply.

Men's Leadership Devotional

⚒ The Forge Weekly Reflection Sheet

Personal Study & Leadership Accountability Questions

1. **Theme in My Life: This week's theme was**
   "_____"
   In my current life, I see this theme at work in the area of:
   "_____
   _____"

2. **Key Verse Insight: The Scripture that stood out most to me this week was:**
   "_____
   _____"

3. *Because it reminded/taught/convicted me that:*
   "_____
   _____
   _____
   _____"

4. **Connection—The story of _____ made me think about:**
   "_____
   _____"

5. *A similar situation in my life has been:*
   "_____
   _____
   _____"

410 The Forge

6. **God's Prompting: One way I feel God is prompting me to grow or change this week is:**
   "_____
   _____
   _____
   _____"

7. **Action Step: As a man of faith and leadership, one practical step I will take this week is:**
   "_____
   _____
   _____
   _____"

8. **Prayer Focus: I sense the need to bring this to God in prayer:**
   "_____
   _____
   _____
   _____"

9. *I also want to lift up these specific people or situations:*
   "_____
   _____
   _____
   _____"

10. **Brotherhood Check-in:**
    One truth I need to share or process with another man is:
    "_____
    _____
    _____
    _____"

11. I plan to connect with: _____ by (day/time): _____

12. Refining at The Forge:
    This week, God is shaping me most in the area of:
    "_____
    _____
    _____
    _____"

13. *I want to remain faithful in this process by:*
    "_____
    _____
    _____
    _____"

Week 50
Creating Safe Spaces

Fostering environments where individuals feel safe to express themselves and seek help.

Cultivating Safe Spaces with Compassion and Support

Henry was a dedicated men's ministry leader at his church, passionate about helping others grow in their faith. He led a weekly Bible study group, filled with men from different walks of life—some were new believers, others had been in the church for years, and a few were just searching for answers. While the group was generally open and friendly, Henry noticed that when deeper, personal topics came up, the atmosphere often grew tense. Many of the men were hesitant to share their struggles, fearful of being judged or misunderstood.

One evening, as the group gathered, Henry sensed that something was weighing heavily on one of the newer members, Chris. Chris was usually quiet, but that night, he looked particularly burdened. When Henry asked how everyone was doing, Chris hesitated, staring at his coffee cup. Henry gently prompted him, "Chris, we're here for you, man. Whatever's on your heart, you're not alone."

Chris took a deep breath and finally spoke up. "Honestly, I've been struggling a lot. Work's been rough, and things at home aren't much better. I feel like I'm failing as a husband and a father, and I don't know what to do." The room fell silent. It was clear that Chris was opening up about something deeply personal, and Henry knew this was a pivotal moment.

Remembering Proverbs 17:17, "A friend loves at all times, and a brother is born for adversity," Henry understood the importance of showing unconditional support. He leaned forward and said, "Chris, thank you for sharing that. It takes courage to be honest about what you're going through, and we're here to walk with you through this. None of us have it all together, but we can bear each other's burdens."

Henry's reference to Galatians 6:2, "Bear one another's burdens, and so fulfill the law of Christ," set the tone for the group. It was a reminder that they were not just a Bible study; they were a brotherhood, called to support one another through the highs and lows of life. As Henry spoke, other men in the group began to share their own struggles—stories of stress, doubts, and fears that had been silently weighing them down. One by one, they realized they were not alone in their battles.

Henry's commitment to creating a safe space transformed the group dynamic. He encouraged the men to not only share but also to actively listen without judgment. He made sure that each person felt heard and valued, emphasizing that this was a place of grace, where they could be honest without fear of condemnation.

Over time, the group became a sanctuary for the men, a place where vulnerability was met with compassion and practical support. They started praying for each other more intentionally, checking in during the week, and offering help beyond the weekly meetings. Some began meeting one-on-one for coffee to talk things through, while others offered practical assistance like babysitting, job networking, or simply being a listening ear late at night.

One day, Chris approached Henry after a particularly moving session. "I just want to thank you," he said, his voice cracking. "This group has been a lifeline for me. I didn't think I'd find a place where I could be real without feeling judged. You guys have shown me what real brotherhood looks like."

Henry smiled, knowing that this was exactly what the group was meant to be—a living expression of Christ's love. He realized that by fostering an environment where men could be honest about their struggles, they were fulfilling the law of Christ in a deeply tangible way. Henry continued to encourage openness, reminding the group that every shared burden lightened the load for someone else and that every act of kindness was a reflection of God's grace.

Henry's leadership in creating a safe space didn't just help the men find support; it deepened their relationships with God and each other. By embodying the principles of Proverbs 17:17 and Galatians 6:2, Henry showed that true leadership is not about having all the answers but about being present, compassionate, and willing to walk alongside others in their journey.

The group's transformation became a testament to the power of empathy and support, inspiring other ministry leaders to cultivate similar environments within their own circles. Henry's commitment to creating safe spaces was a reminder that when we bear one another's burdens and love each other through adversity, we create communities that reflect the heart of Christ.

Through his efforts, Henry helped build a brotherhood that not only uplifted each other but also served as a powerful witness of God's love to those who came searching for a place where they could truly belong.

416 The Forge

> Old Testament: Proverbs 17:17 "A friend loves at all times, and a brother is born for adversity."
>
> New Testament: Galatians 6:2 "Bear one another's burdens, and so fulfill the law of Christ."

As Christian men, we have a vital role in creating safe spaces where others can express themselves openly and seek help without fear of judgment. Proverbs 17:17 highlights the unwavering love of a true friend, reminding us that authentic brotherhood shines brightest during times of adversity. In Galatians 6:2, we are called to bear one another's burdens, fulfilling the law of Christ through our support and compassion. Let us strive to cultivate environments marked by trust, where vulnerability is met with understanding and encouragement. By embodying these principles, we can foster relationships that not only uplift others but also deepen our own faith and commitment to Christ, demonstrating His love in tangible ways.

⚒ The Forge Weekly Reflection Sheet

Personal Study & Leadership Accountability Questions

1. **Theme in My Life: This week's theme was**
   "_____"

   In my current life, I see this theme at work in the area of:
   "_____
   _____"

2. **Key Verse Insight: The Scripture that stood out most to me this week was:**
   "_____
   _____"

3. ***Because it reminded/taught/convicted me that:***
   "_____
   _____
   _____
   _____"

4. **Connection—The story of _____ made me think about:**
   "_____
   _____"

5. ***A similar situation in my life has been:***
   "_____
   _____
   _____
   _____"

6. **God's Prompting:** One way I feel God is prompting me to grow or change this week is:
   "_____
   _____
   _____
   _____"

7. **Action Step:** As a man of faith and leadership, one practical step I will take this week is:
   "_____
   _____
   _____
   _____"

8. **Prayer Focus:** I sense the need to bring this to God in prayer:
   "_____
   _____
   _____
   _____"

9. *I also want to lift up these specific people or situations:*
   "_____
   _____
   _____
   _____"

10. **Brotherhood Check-in:**
    One truth I need to share or process with another man is:
    "_____
    _____
    _____
    _____"

11. I plan to connect with: _____ by (day/time): _____

12. **Refining at The Forge:**
    This week, God is shaping me most in the area of:
    "_____
    _____
    _____
    _____"

13. *I want to remain faithful in this process by:*
    "_____
    _____
    _____
    _____"

Week 51
Navigating Change

Leading through change with wisdom, compassion, and a focus on God's guidance.

Leading Through Change with Faith and Wisdom

Dennis had been the director of operations at his company for over a decade, known for his steady leadership and commitment to his team. His clear vision and dependable nature had guided the company through various ups and downs, earning him the respect of both his peers and subordinates. But recently, the company was facing significant challenges—a shift in market dynamics, new technologies, and evolving customer demands were forcing them to rethink their entire business strategy. The board announced a major restructuring, and Dennis found himself navigating a season of change that felt overwhelming.

One morning, Dennis sat in his office, feeling the weight of uncertainty. He opened his Bible and found himself reading Ecclesiastes 3:1: "For everything there is a season, and a time for every matter under heaven." The words reminded him that change was a natural part of life, and that every season, no matter how difficult, had a purpose. He realized that resisting change was not an option; instead, he needed to embrace it with a spirit of openness, trusting that God was in control.

The Forge

Determined to lead his team through this transition, Dennis also turned to Romans 12:2: "Do not be conformed to this world, but be transformed by the renewal of your mind..." He knew that leading through change required more than just strategic thinking; it demanded a renewed mindset anchored in God's wisdom. Dennis began to pray daily, asking for guidance, clarity, and the strength to make decisions that would honor God and support his team.

Dennis gathered his team for a meeting, not just to discuss the logistical changes but to address the fears and concerns that everyone was feeling. He spoke candidly about the challenges ahead, but instead of focusing solely on the problems, he highlighted the opportunities for growth and innovation. "Change can be tough," Dennis acknowledged, "but it's also a chance for us to rethink how we work, to become better, more adaptable, and to find new ways to serve our customers and each other."

He encouraged his team to share their thoughts and ideas, creating a space where everyone felt heard. Dennis knew that navigating change wasn't just about implementing new strategies; it was about leading with compassion and understanding the human side of the transition. He reminded them that, like any season, this too would pass, and their strength would come from facing it together.

As the restructuring unfolded, Dennis made it a point to stay connected with his team on a personal level. He checked in regularly, not just on their work but on how they were coping with the changes. He offered support, prayer, and practical help, embodying the wisdom of Ecclesiastes 3:1 by embracing each moment as an opportunity to grow and learn. Dennis's calm, steady presence became a source of comfort, reminding his team that even in uncertainty, they were not alone.

Throughout the process, Dennis also sought counsel from his church community, recognizing the importance of surrounding himself with wise, godly voices. He joined a small group of other business leaders, where they discussed navigating change from a biblical perspective. This fellowship strengthened his resolve, and he brought the lessons he learned back to his workplace, reinforcing the importance of faith, resilience, and adaptability.

As the months passed, the company slowly adjusted to the new structure. There were bumps along the way, but Dennis's leadership helped guide his team through the storm. They not only adapted but thrived, finding new rhythms and discovering fresh ways to excel. Dennis's willingness to embrace change with wisdom, compassion, and a focus on God's guidance had set the tone for the entire organization.

One day, after successfully landing a major new client, one of Dennis's team members approached him. "Dennis, I just wanted to thank you," he said. "This whole process has been tough, but you never wavered. You reminded us that even in change, there's hope, and that made all the difference."

Dennis smiled, humbled by the acknowledgment. He knew that his strength didn't come from his own abilities but from trusting in God's timing and guidance. By leading with a renewed mind, as Romans 12:2 encouraged, Dennis had helped his team not only survive a season of change but embrace it as an opportunity for transformation.

Dennis's journey through this challenging season was a powerful example of what it means to lead with faith. By leaning into God's wisdom and showing compassion to those around him, he demonstrated that change, though often difficult, can be navigated with grace and purpose.

424 The Forge

His story reminded everyone that when we trust in God's plan and adapt with an open heart, we become beacons of hope, ready for whatever lies ahead.

> Old Testament: Ecclesiastes 3:1 "For everything there is a season, and a time for every matter under heaven."
>
> New Testament: Romans 12:2 "Do not be conformed to this world, but be transformed by the renewal of your mind..."

As Christian men, we often face seasons of change that can be challenging to navigate. Ecclesiastes 3:1 reminds us that there is a time for everything, encouraging us to embrace each season with the understanding that God is sovereign over every transition. In Romans 12:2, we are called to renew our minds and resist being shaped by the pressures of the world around us. Let us lead through change with wisdom and compassion, seeking God's guidance in prayer and Scripture. By anchoring ourselves in His truth, we can adapt to new circumstances while remaining steadfast in our mission. May we be beacons of hope and strength to those around us, trusting that God is at work in every moment of change, preparing us for what lies ahead.

⚒ The Forge Weekly Reflection Sheet

Personal Study & Leadership Accountability Questions

1. **Theme in My Life: This week's theme was**
   "_____"

   In my current life, I see this theme at work in the area of:
   "_____
   _____"

2. **Key Verse Insight: The Scripture that stood out most to me this week was:**
   "_____
   _____"

3. *Because it reminded/taught/convicted me that:*
   "_____
   _____
   _____
   _____"

4. **Connection—The story of _____ made me think about:**
   "_____
   _____"

5. *A similar situation in my life has been:*
   "_____
   _____
   _____
   _____"

6. **God's Prompting:** One way I feel God is prompting me to grow or change this week is:
   "_____
   _____
   _____
   _____"

7. **Action Step:** As a man of faith and leadership, one practical step I will take this week is:
   "_____
   _____
   _____
   _____"

8. **Prayer Focus:** I sense the need to bring this to God in prayer:
   "_____
   _____
   _____
   _____"

9. *I also want to lift up these specific people or situations:*
   "_____
   _____
   _____
   _____"

10. **Brotherhood Check-in:**
    One truth I need to share or process with another man is:
    "_____
    _____
    _____
    _____"

11. I plan to connect with: _____ **by (day/time):** _____

12. Refining at The Forge:
   This week, God is shaping me most in the area of:
   "_____
   _____
   _____
   _____"

13. *I want to remain faithful in this process by:*
   "_____
   _____
   _____
   _____"

Week 52
Faithfulness in Small Things

Being diligent and faithful in small responsibilities, knowing they lead to greater opportunities.

In a small town, a young man named Jerry worked as a custodian in the local church. Each day, he arrived early, sweeping the floors, dusting the pews, and ensuring the sanctuary was ready for worship. While some might see such tasks as menial, Jerry approached them with a heart full of purpose, believing that every small act contributed to God's greater plan. He often recalled Zechariah 4:10, "For whoever has despised the day of small things shall rejoice," finding joy in his role, even when no one was watching.

One Sunday, after service, the pastor approached Jerry with a smile. "I've noticed how well you care for this place. Would you be interested in helping with our youth group? I believe your heart for service would inspire the kids." Jerry felt a rush of excitement but also nervousness. This was a greater responsibility, but he remembered Luke 16:10, which reminded him that "one who is faithful in a very little is also faithful in much."

Accepting the challenge, Jerry began mentoring the youth, sharing his faith and experiences. He found fulfillment in encouraging young men to embrace their own small responsibilities, just as he had. As the months passed, his influence grew, and he helped launch a community outreach program that served the less fortunate in their town.

Through it all, Jerry reflected on how his diligence in small tasks had opened doors he never expected. His faithfulness had not only enriched his own life but had also transformed the lives of others. In those small beginnings, he discovered the joy of serving God, knowing that each humble act was part of a larger tapestry woven by the Creator's hand.

> Old Testament: Zechariah 4:10 "For whoever has despised the day of small things shall rejoice..."
>
> New Testament: Luke 16:10 "One who is faithful in a very little is also faithful in much..."

As Christian men, we are called to embrace faithfulness in the small things, recognizing that diligence in our everyday responsibilities can lead to greater opportunities in God's plan. Zechariah 4:10 reminds us that those who do not despise the day of small beginnings will ultimately rejoice in the fruits of their labor. Similarly, in Luke 16:10, we see that our faithfulness in little things reflects our readiness for greater tasks. Let us cultivate a spirit of perseverance and integrity in our daily duties, knowing that every small act of faithfulness is a building block for God's greater purpose in our lives. May we find joy in these humble beginnings, trusting that our commitment will bear lasting fruit for His kingdom.

⚒ The Forge Weekly Reflection Sheet

Personal Study & Leadership Accountability Questions

1. **Theme in My Life:** This week's theme was
   "_____"

   In my current life, I see this theme at work in the area of:
   "_____
   _____"

2. **Key Verse Insight:** The Scripture that stood out most to me this week was:
   "_____
   _____"

3. **Because it reminded/taught/convicted me that:**
   "_____
   _____
   _____
   _____"

4. **Connection**—The story of _____ made me think about:
   "_____
   _____"

5. *A similar situation in my life has been:*
   "_____
   _____
   _____
   _____"

6. **God's Prompting: One way I feel God is prompting me to grow or change this week is:**
   "_____
   _____
   _____
   _____ "

7. **Action Step: As a man of faith and leadership, one practical step I will take this week is:**
   "_____
   _____
   _____
   _____ "

8. **Prayer Focus: I sense the need to bring this to God in prayer:**
   "_____
   _____
   _____
   _____ "

9. *I also want to lift up these specific people or situations:*
   "_____
   _____
   _____
   _____ "

10. **Brotherhood Check-in:**
    One truth I need to share or process with another man is:
    "_____
    _____
    _____
    _____ "

11. I plan to connect with: _____ by (day/time): _____

12. Refining at The Forge:
    This week, God is shaping me most in the area of:
    "_____
    _____
    _____
    _____"

13. *I want to remain faithful in this process by:*
    "_____
    _____
    _____
    _____"

The Final Ember

A Call to Go Forth

You have walked the yearlong path. Week by week, line upon line, precept upon precept—you've been shaped in the fire. You've wrestled with truth, owned your weakness, deepened your faith, and sharpened your purpose. Now, standing at the edge of this devotional forge, you are not who you were when you began.

You are a man *formed* by the Word, *tested* in reflection, and *readied* for impact.

But *this* is not the finish line. This is the beginning of something greater. What God has forged in the quiet places of your heart must now be lived out in the noise of the world. You are not called to simply admire the shape you've taken. You are called to wield it. To lead with it. To protect, provide, proclaim, and persevere with it.

Now is the time to rise.

As Paul commissioned Timothy, so now we commission you (2 Timothy 4:1–2):

"I charge you in the presence of God and of Christ Jesus... preach the word; be ready in season and out of season; reprove, rebuke, and exhort, with complete patience and teaching."

You are a covenant man. You are a kingdom leader. You have been forged for such a time as this.

436 The Forge

So now, we consecrate you—not to ease or comfort, but to courage and character. Not to retreat, but to responsibility. Not to blend in, but to stand out as salt and light in a fading world.

> *May your leadership be sacrificial.*
> *May your words be true.*
> *May your marriage be a refuge.*
> *May your children rise and call you blessed.*
> *May your community know Christ because you walk among them.*

And when the fire comes again—and it will—may it only refine what God has already begun.

Welcome, brother. You've passed through the Forge.

Now go!
Lead boldly!
Live faithfully!
Die empty!

For the King and His kingdom!

— THE —
FORGE
WHERE MEN ARE SHAPED
FOR PURPOSE

Leader's Addendum:
Weekly Discussion Prompts

If you are leading a Forge discussion group, below are some useful questions to help prompt your men into discussion. Each week speaks to one of the six core themes, with a focus on one of the sub-themes outlined below. Feel free to add or use any other insights you might feel the Holy Spirit is suggesting. Remember, this journey is one of mutual discovery. Your role is to help others discover, while you yourself does the same.

Theme 1: Foundations of Godly Manhood (Weeks 1–9)

Central Focus: Internal character, submission to God, emotional maturity, and relational stability.

Week 1–3: Spiritual Alignment – Yielding to God, Serving, Vision

- Week 1 – Yielding to God's Authority

  When have you found it hardest to trust God's authority in your life? What was the result of leaning on your own understanding?

  How can we practically submit to God's leadership in areas like work, relationships, and daily decision-making?

  In what ways can godly submission actually make a man *stronger*, not weaker?

- Week 2 – Faithful Servanthood

Jesus said He came "not to be served, but to serve." What does that kind of servanthood look like in a man's daily life?

What personal obstacles (pride, busyness, fatigue) keep you from serving others with consistency?

Share a time when someone's quiet act of service deeply impacted you. What did it teach you about leadership?

- Week 3 – Visionary Leadership

God calls leaders to "write the vision." What vision has God been stirring in you for your family, church, or workplace?

What's the difference between a God-given vision and a self-driven ambition?

How do we help other men "run with" the vision God gives us?

Week 4–7: Core Character – Integrity, Courage, Mentorship, Emotional Intelligence

- Week 4 – Integrity and Honesty

Integrity is what you do when no one is watching. What is one area of life where you've struggled to live with integrity?

How can a man recover trust once it's been broken? What role does transparency play in leadership?

What's one decision you've made recently that reflects your commitment to biblical integrity?

- Week 5 – Courage in Adversity

  Where in your life is God calling you to be courageous right now?

  How do fear and faith battle for control when life gets hard? What helps you stay anchored?

  Share a story when someone else's courage in Christ inspired you to act boldly.

- Week 6 – Discipleship and Mentorship

  Who has discipled or mentored you in your walk with Christ, and what lasting impact did that have?

  What's the difference between simply giving advice and truly investing in someone spiritually?

  Is God prompting you to begin mentoring someone? What might be holding you back?

- Week 7 – Emotional Intelligence

  How do you typically respond when emotions—yours or others'—get intense? Do you lead from reaction or reflection?

  What does it look like to lead your home or team with emotional maturity, especially when tension is high?

  How can developing emotional intelligence help men become more Christlike in relationships?

Week 8–9: Leadership in Relationship – Conflict Resolution, Prayerful Leadership

- Week 8 – Conflict Resolution

How do you typically handle conflict—avoidance, aggression, or seeking peace?

Share a time when you witnessed or participated in a conflict that was resolved well. What made it work?

What specific steps can Christian men take to become peacemakers in their homes, churches, and communities?

- Week 9 – Prayerful Leadership

What's your current relationship with prayer when making decisions? Do you consult God first—or after things fall apart?

How has prayer shaped or changed your leadership in any area of your life?

What would it look like for our group to grow in shared, intentional prayer for one another?

Theme 2: Stewardship of Life (Weeks 10–15)

Focus: Managing what God has entrusted—money, family, work, and community.

Week 10: Financial Stewardship

- Week 10 – Financial Stewardship

How do you currently view the money God has entrusted to you: possession, tool, or responsibility?

What challenges do you face in practicing generosity or financial integrity?

How can men support each other in being wise stewards—without shame or pride—through accountability and example?

Week 11–13: Family Leadership – Home, Husband, Father

- Week 11 – Family as a Priority

  What are some signs that your family might be getting your leftovers instead of your best?

  How do you balance being both a spiritual leader and an emotionally present husband and father?

  What's one practical change you could make this week to prioritize your family more intentionally?

- Week 12 – Role of the Husband

  How do you understand the biblical command to "love your wife as Christ loved the church"? What does that look like daily?

  What are some obstacles that keep men from leading their marriages with humility and grace?

  In what ways does sacrificial love strengthen both leadership and intimacy in marriage?

- Week 13 – Fatherhood and Guidance

  How do you currently guide your children spiritually? What intentional habits do you want to start or strengthen?

  What does "not provoking your children to anger" look like in real-life parenting?

How has your own experience of being fathered shaped how you lead as a father today?

Week 14–15: Workplace and Community – Vocational Integrity, Civic Engagement

- Week 14 – Integrity in the Workplace

  Where is it most tempting to compromise your integrity in professional life—and why?

  How does working "as for the Lord" shift your attitude toward daily tasks or difficult situations?

  Share a time when doing the right thing at work came at a cost. What did you learn from it?

- Week 15 – Community Engagement

  What does it mean to "seek the welfare of your city" in your current context?

  Where are you currently involved—or feeling called—to serve outside your home and church?

  How can our group model community engagement that reflects Christ's heart for the forgotten and overlooked?

Theme 3: Mission and Witness (Weeks 16–20)

Focus: Evangelism, accountability, spiritual endurance, and moral courage.

Week 16: Evangelism

- **Week 16 – Witnessing and Evangelism**

What holds you back from sharing your faith more openly with others?

How do you balance living as a quiet witness with actively proclaiming the gospel?

Who is one person in your life that God may be calling you to gently pursue with spiritual intention?

Week 17: Accountability

- Week 17 – Accountability and Transparency

What's the difference between confession and accountability—and why do we often avoid both?

Who in your life has permission to ask you hard questions—and how often do you talk?

How can this group grow in becoming a place of grace, honesty, and brotherly sharpening?

Week 18–20: Patience, Service, Ethics

- Week 18 – Patience and Understanding

    In what types of situations do you most often lose patience? What tends to trigger your frustration?

    How has someone else's patience helped shape your character or restore your confidence?

    What would it look like to lead your home, team, or community with grace this week?

- Week 19 – Cultivating a Servant Heart

    When do you find yourself serving for recognition instead of for love? What does that reveal?

How does Jesus' act of washing feet reshape your understanding of leadership?

Where is God calling you to serve in a quieter or more sacrificial way right now?

- Week 20 – Moral and Ethical Leadership

When facing a moral gray area, what filters or decision-making processes do you rely on?

How do we help each other stay upright in a culture that often rewards compromise?

What are some modern examples of moral courage—and how can we train ourselves to act with integrity under pressure?

Theme 4: Relational and Social Influence (Weeks 21–30)

Focus: Marriage, children, worship, temptation, trust-building, and social impact.

Week 21–23: Household Roles – Children, Balance, Marriage

- Week 21 – Raising Godly Children

What does it practically mean to "train up a child in the way he should go" in today's culture?

How do you handle your failures as a father without slipping into shame or passivity?

What are one or two habits that could help you be more intentional in your child's spiritual formation?

- Week 22 – Balancing Work and Family

What warning signs show up when your life is out of balance?

How do you discern between godly responsibility and unhealthy overcommitment?

What boundaries could you set to protect what matters most?

- Week 23 – Supportive Partnership in Marriage

  In what ways can a husband *support* his wife without controlling or withdrawing?

  How do you and your spouse make space to hear and value each other's spiritual gifts and goals?

  How does mutual submission, as taught in Scripture, enhance your role as a leader?

Week 24–25: Spiritual Discipline – Worship, Temptation

- Week 24 – Leadership in Worship

  How do you model worship in your home—personally and as a spiritual leader?

  What does it mean for a man to lead not just in prayer or song, but with a worshipful lifestyle?

  How can our group encourage each other to worship with authenticity—not just routine?

- Week 25 – Overcoming Temptation

  Where are you most vulnerable to temptation right now—and who knows about it?

What patterns help you resist temptation, and what patterns make it easier to fall?

How can we support one another in practical ways when temptation hits hard?

Week 26–30: Social Maturity – Honor, Communication, Diversity, Service, Resilience

- Week 26 – Fostering a Culture of Honor

  How do you define honor in a world that often rewards disrespect and sarcasm?

  Who in your life needs to be honored more—whether through words, actions, or attitude?

  How can we build a brotherhood that calls men up through encouragement, not shame?

- Week 27 – Listening and Communication

  Are you more prone to speak quickly or to listen carefully? How does that affect your leadership?

  What would it look like to become a more attentive listener in your marriage, friendships, or workplace?

  What's one recent conversation where you wish you had listened more fully—what can you learn from it?

- Week 28 – Embracing Diversity

  What biases—spoken or unspoken—might keep you from loving or learning from someone different than you?

How does biblical unity differ from cultural uniformity?

How can men lead in building bridges within the Church, home, and community?

- Week 29 – Service to the Vulnerable

Who in your world would be considered "the least of these," and how are you showing up for them?

What stops Christian men from engaging with the broken or marginalized in their communities?

What role does humility play in serving others who can't repay you?

- Week 30 – Resilience in Leadership

What's an area of life right now where you feel spiritually or emotionally worn down?

How has God used failure or hardship to strengthen you as a leader?

What does it look like to press on with joy and faith when results are slow or unseen?

Theme 5: Spiritual Legacy and Interior Life (Weeks 31–40)

Focus: Joy, rest, personal discipline, and living a life that outlasts you.

Week 31–33: Inner Life – Legacy, Joy, Gratitude

- Week 31 – Building a Legacy of Faith

What do you hope your children, spouse, or friends will say about your faith after you're gone?

Are there any habits or patterns in your life right now that could undermine the legacy you want to leave?

Who modeled a godly legacy for you—and what did they pass on?

- Week 32 – The Role of Humor and Joy

  How can laughter and joy become spiritual disciplines instead of distractions?

  When is the last time you truly laughed or enjoyed rest without guilt?

  What are ways Christian men can lead with lightness without losing depth?

- Week 33 – Gratitude and Contentment

  What are the biggest threats to your contentment right now—comparison, ambition, entitlement?

  How does regularly practicing gratitude shift your perspective as a leader?

  What's one thing you've taken for granted lately that you want to thank God for today?

Week 34–35: Sabbath and Justice

- Week 34 – Sabbath Rest

  How do you typically view rest—as reward, inconvenience, or weakness?

What prevents you from truly honoring a Sabbath rhythm in your week?

What would your life look like if you regularly made space for sacred rest and reflection?

- Week 35 – Social Responsibility

    In what ways do you see injustice or brokenness in your local community—and what's your role in it?

    How can Christian men lead with both truth and compassion when it comes to social issues?

    What does it mean to carry responsibility for your "neighbor" in a modern world?

Week 36–40: Intentionality, Apologetics, Reliability, Endurance, Criticism

- Week 36 – Intentionality in Relationships

    Which relationships in your life are you currently coasting in—and why?

    What does it look like to pursue friendships and family ties with spiritual purpose, not just social comfort?

    Who is God calling you to initiate with this week—and what's stopping you?

- Week 37 – Apologetics and Defense of Faith

    What's your greatest fear when it comes to defending your faith in conversation?

    How can you grow in knowledge without becoming argumentative or prideful?

What's one truth about the gospel that you want to be able to explain more clearly?

- Week 38 – Building Trust and Reliability

    Do others consider you reliable? Where might there be cracks in your consistency?

    What's the connection between showing up, following through, and earning spiritual authority?

    How can you rebuild trust where it's been broken?

- Week 39 – Endurance in Trials

    What trial are you walking through (or have walked through) that has tested your endurance?

    How do you usually respond to long seasons of waiting, pain, or uncertainty?

    What does it mean to endure *with hope* rather than just survive?

- Week 40 – Responding to Criticism

    When have you reacted poorly to correction—and what did that reveal about your heart?

    How can godly men use criticism as a tool for growth, not shame?

    What helps you tell the difference between helpful feedback and harmful voices?

Theme 6: Leadership in Community and Culture
(Weeks 41–52)

Focus: Guiding others, defending truth, cultivating unity, adapting to change, and finishing strong.

Week 41–43: Influence and Gifts – Unity, Truth, Spiritual Gifts

- Week 41 – Promoting Peace and Unity

  What role do you typically play in conflict—peacemaker, avoider, or agitator?

  What's one relationship where you need to be more intentional about building unity?

  How can Christian men lead the way in healing divisions within their homes, churches, or communities?

- Week 42 – Advocating for the Truth

  What truths are you tempted to stay silent about because of fear or cultural pressure?

  How do you balance grace and truth in conversations with people who disagree with you?

  Where is God calling you to speak up with courage this week?

- Week 43 – Utilizing Spiritual Gifts

    Do you know your spiritual gifts? How are you actively using them right now?

    What stops you from stepping more boldly into your God-given calling?

    How can we as a group help one another recognize and activate our gifts for the kingdom?

Week 44–46: Boundaries, Worship, Church Leadership

- Week 44 – Healthy Boundaries

    Where are your boundaries too loose—or too rigid—and how is that affecting your relationships?

    What does Jesus teach us about saying no, withdrawing, or protecting time and energy?

    How can setting boundaries help you serve others *more faithfully*, not less?

- Week 45 – Living a Life of Worship

    What parts of your life feel disconnected from worship right now?

    How can you express worship beyond singing—through work, marriage, habits, or service?

    What helps shift your focus from routine to reverence in daily life?

- Week 46 – Supporting Church Leadership

    What is your current attitude toward the leadership in your church—honoring, critical, disengaged?

How can men come alongside pastors and elders with strength, service, and encouragement?

What's one small but meaningful way you can support your church this month?

Week 47–49: Vision, Compassion, Lifelong Learning

- Week 47 – Long-Term Vision

    Are you leading your life with long-term vision or short-term reactions?

    What legacy are your current habits building—personally, spiritually, relationally?

    What might God be asking you to invest in today that won't bear fruit until much later?

- Week 48 – Empathy and Compassion

    What does it mean to lead with empathy without compromising truth?

    How can men become more emotionally available without becoming emotionally reactive?

    Who in your life needs compassion more than correction right now?

- Week 49 – Promoting Lifelong Learning

    When's the last time you truly learned something that changed how you live?

    Are you coasting on old knowledge or actively growing in wisdom and skill?

    What disciplines can help men keep a learner's heart for life?

Week 50–52: Safe Culture, Navigating Change, Small Faithful Acts

- Week 50 – Creating Safe Spaces

  Do people feel emotionally and spiritually safe around you? Why or why not?

  What role do confession, grace, and listening play in creating trust?

  How can our group become a place where men show up fully, not just perform?

- Week 51 – Navigating Change

  What changes are you currently resisting, and what might God be doing through them?

  How can men lead their families and churches with steadiness in seasons of transition?

  What biblical truths help anchor you when the future feels uncertain?

- Week 52 – Faithfulness in Small Things

  What "small things" in your life feel unseen or unimportant—but may be shaping your character?

  How can daily faithfulness prepare you for future opportunities and spiritual leadership?

  How does God measure success differently than the world does—and how should that affect your decisions?

Scriptures for weekly topics

1. Yielding to God's Authority
   Old Testament:
        Proverbs 3:5-6
        Isaiah 45:9
   New Testament:
        Matthew 6:33
        Romans 13:1-2
        James 4:7
        1 Peter 5:6
        Philippians 2:9-11
        Colossians 3:17
        Hebrews 13:17

2. Faithful Servanthood
   Old Testament:
        1 Samuel 12:24
        Micah 6:8
   New Testament:
        Matthew 20:26-28
        John 12:26
        Philippians 2:5-7
        1 Peter 4:10
        Romans 12:11
        Colossians 3:23-24
        Titus 2:9-10

3. Visionary Leadership
   Old Testament:
        Habakkuk 2:2-3
        Nehemiah 2:17-18
   New Testament:
        Acts 20:28
        1 Corinthians 12:28
        Ephesians 4:11-12
        Philippians 3:13-14
        1 Timothy 4:12
        2 Timothy 1:7

- Hebrews 13:7

4. Integrity and Honesty

Old Testament:
- Proverbs 11:3
- Psalm 25:21

New Testament:
- 2 Corinthians 8:21
- Ephesians 4:25
- Philippians 4:8
- Colossians 3:9
- 1 Peter 3:16
- Titus 2:7-8
- 1 Thessalonians 4:11-12

5. Courage in Adversity

Old Testament:
- Joshua 1:9
- Isaiah 41:10

New Testament:
- John 16:33
- Romans 8:31
- 2 Corinthians 4:8-9
- Ephesians 6:10-11
- Philippians 1:28
- 2 Timothy 1:7
- Hebrews 10:35

6. Discipleship and Mentorship

Old Testament:
- Proverbs 27:17
- Deuteronomy 6:6-7

New Testament:
- Matthew 28:19-20
- Mark 3:14
- Acts 11:25-26
- 2 Timothy 2:2
- 1 Corinthians 4:16-17
- Titus 1:9
- Hebrews 10:24

7. Emotional Intelligence
   Old Testament:
      Proverbs 16:32
      Psalm 139:23-24
   New Testament:
      James 1:19-20
      Galatians 5:22-23
      Colossians 3:12
      Romans 12:15
      1 Peter 3:8
      Ephesians 4:26-27
      Philippians 2:3-4

8. Conflict Resolution
   Old Testament:
      Proverbs 15:1
      Genesis 13:8-9
   New Testament:
      Matthew 18:15-17
      Romans 12:18
      Colossians 3:13
      Ephesians 4:31-32
      James 3:17-18
      1 Corinthians 6:1-7
      Philippians 4:2-3

9. Prayerful Leadership
   Old Testament:
      Nehemiah 1:4-11
      Daniel 6:10
   New Testament:
      Luke 5:16
      Acts 6:4
      Ephesians 6:18
      1 Timothy 2:1-2
      Colossians 4:2
      James 5:16
      1 Thessalonians 5:17

10. Financial Stewardship
Old Testament:
- Proverbs 3:9-10
- Malachi 3:10

New Testament:
- Matthew 6:19-21
- Luke 16:10-11
- 1 Timothy 6:10
- 2 Corinthians 9:6-7
- Hebrews 13:5
- Acts 20:35
- Philippians 4:19

11. Family as a Priority
Old Testament:
- Deuteronomy 6:6-7
- Proverbs 22:6

New Testament:
- Ephesians 6:1-4
- 1 Timothy 5:8
- Colossians 3:18-21
- 1 Peter 3:7
- Titus 2:4-5
- Matthew 19:19
- Luke 2:51

12. Role of the Husband
Old Testament:
- Genesis 2:24
- Proverbs 5:18-19

New Testament:
- Ephesians 5:25
- Colossians 3:19
- 1 Peter 3:7
- 1 Corinthians 7:3-4
- 1 Timothy 5:8
- Titus 2:2
- Matthew 19:5

13. Fatherhood and Guidance
Old Testament:
- Psalm 103:13
- Proverbs 3:12

New Testament:
- Ephesians 6:4
- Colossians 3:21
- Hebrews 12:7
- 1 Thessalonians 2:11-12
- Luke 11:11-13
- 1 Corinthians 4:14-15
- James 1:5

14. Integrity in the Workplace
Old Testament:
- Proverbs 10:9
- Ecclesiastes 9:10

New Testament:
- Colossians 3:23-24
- 1 Thessalonians 4:11-12
- Ephesians 6:5-8
- Titus 2:7-8
- 1 Peter 2:12
- Philippians 2:14-15
- Romans 12:17

15. Community Engagement
Old Testament:
- Leviticus 19:18
- Jeremiah 29:7

New Testament:
- Matthew 5:16
- Romans 12:13
- 1 Peter 4:10
- Galatians 6:2
- Hebrews 13:16
- James 1:27
- 1 John 3:17

16. Witnessing and Evangelism
Old Testament:
- Isaiah 6:8
- Psalm 96:3

New Testament:
- Matthew 28:19-20
- Mark 16:15
- Acts 1:8
- Romans 10:14-15
- 2 Corinthians 5:20
- 1 Peter 3:15
- Colossians 4:5-6

17. Accountability and Transparency
- **Old Testament:**
  - Proverbs 27:17
  - Ecclesiastes 4:9-10
- **New Testament:**
  - James 5:16
  - Galatians 6:1-2
  - 1 John 1:7
  - Ephesians 5:11
  - Romans 14:12
  - Colossians 3:9
  - 1 Timothy 5:20

18. Patience and Understanding
- **Old Testament:**
  - Proverbs 19:11
  - Psalm 37:7
- **New Testament:**
  - James 1:19
  - 1 Thessalonians 5:14
  - Colossians 3:12-13
  - Ephesians 4:2
  - 2 Timothy 2:24
  - Romans 12:12
  - Philippians 4:5

19. Cultivating a Servant Heart
Old Testament:
- Isaiah 58:10
- Proverbs 11:25

New Testament:
- Mark 10:43-45
- Philippians 2:3-4
- Romans 12:10
- Galatians 5:13
- John 13:14-15
- Colossians 3:23-24
- 1 Peter 5:5

20. Moral and Ethical Leadership
Old Testament:
- Micah 6:8
- Psalm 78:72

New Testament:
- Titus 2:7-8
- 1 Peter 5:3
- 1 Timothy 4:12
- Philippians 2:15
- Ephesians 4:25
- Colossians 3:9
- 2 Corinthians 1:12

21. Raising Godly Children
Old Testament:
- Proverbs 22:6
- Deuteronomy 11:19

New Testament:
- Ephesians 6:4
- Colossians 3:21
- 2 Timothy 3:14-15
- Titus 2:6-7
- Matthew 19:14
- 1 Peter 5:2-3
- Hebrews 12:11

22. Balancing Work and Family
Old Testament:
- Ecclesiastes 3:1
- Proverbs 24:27

New Testament:
- 1 Timothy 3:5
- 1 Corinthians 7:32-34
- Colossians 3:18-21
- Ephesians 6:1-4
- Titus 2:4-5
- Philippians 4:5
- Hebrews 4:9-10

23. Supportive Partnership in Marriage
Old Testament:
- Genesis 2:18
- Ecclesiastes 4:9-12

New Testament:
- Ephesians 5:33
- 1 Corinthians 13:4-7
- 1 Peter 3:1-7
- Colossians 3:18-19
- Matthew 19:6
- Titus 2:3-5
- 1 Timothy 5:14

24. Leadership in Worship
Old Testament:
- Psalm 95:6
- 2 Chronicles 20:21

New Testament:
- John 4:24
- Colossians 3:16
- Hebrews 13:15
- 1 Corinthians 14:26
- Ephesians 5:19-20
- Revelation 4:11
- Romans 12:1

25. Overcoming Temptation
Old Testament:
- Psalm 119:11
- Proverbs 4:14-15

New Testament:
- Matthew 26:41
- 1 Corinthians 10:13
- James 1:12-14
- 1 Peter 5:8-9
- Ephesians 6:11-12
- Hebrews 4:15-16
- Galatians 5:16

26. Fostering a Culture of Honor
Old Testament:
- Exodus 20:12
- Leviticus 19:32

New Testament:
- Romans 12:10
- Philippians 2:3
- 1 Peter 2:17
- Ephesians 6:2
- 1 Timothy 5:17
- Hebrews 13:4
- 1 Thessalonians 5:12-13

27. Listening and Communication
Old Testament:
- Proverbs 18:13
- Ecclesiastes 5:2

New Testament:
- James 1:19
- Colossians 4:6
- Ephesians 4:29
- Matthew 12:36-37
- 1 Peter 3:15
- Titus 3:2
- Proverbs 15:1

28. Embracing Diversity
Old Testament:
- Genesis 1:27
- Isaiah 56:7

New Testament:
- Galatians 3:28
- Colossians 3:11
- Romans 12:4-5
- 1 Corinthians 12:12-13
- Ephesians 2:14
- James 2:1-4
- Revelation 7:9

29. Service to the Vulnerable
Old Testament:
- Isaiah 1:17
- Proverbs 31:8-9

New Testament:
- James 1:27
- Matthew 25:35-36
- Galatians 6:2
- Romans 12:13
- 1 John 3:17
- 1 Peter 4:10
- Hebrews 13:16

30. Resilience in Leadership
Old Testament:
- Isaiah 40:31
- Nehemiah 4:14

New Testament:
- 2 Corinthians 4:8-9
- Galatians 6:9
- Philippians 4:13
- 1 Peter 5:10
- Romans 5:3-4
- 2 Timothy 2:3
- James 1:12

31. Building a Legacy of Faith
Old Testament:
- Deuteronomy 6:5-7
- Psalm 145:4

New Testament:
- 2 Timothy 1:5
- Hebrews 11:1-2
- 1 Peter 1:7
- Philippians 4:9
- Colossians 1:9-10
- 1 Thessalonians 1:3
- 2 Peter 1:5-8

32. The Role of Humor and Joy
Old Testament:
- Proverbs 17:22
- Ecclesiastes 3:4

New Testament:
- Philippians 4:4
- 1 Thessalonians 5:16
- Romans 15:13
- James 1:2
- Galatians 5:22
- 1 Peter 1:8
- Luke 6:21

33. Gratitude and Contentment
Old Testament:
- Psalm 100:4
- Proverbs 15:16

New Testament:
- Philippians 4:11-13
- Colossians 3:15-17
- 1 Thessalonians 5:18
- Hebrews 13:5
- 1 Timothy 6:6-8
- Ephesians 5:20
- James 1:17

34. Sabbath Rest
Old Testament:
Exodus 20:8-10
Isaiah 58:13-14
New Testament:
Matthew 11:28-30
Mark 2:27
Hebrews 4:9-10
Luke 6:5
Colossians 2:16-17
Romans 14:5-6
1 Peter 5:7

35. Social Responsibility
Old Testament:
Micah 6:8
Isaiah 58:6-7
New Testament:
Matthew 5:13-16
Romans 12:9-13
James 2:14-17
1 Timothy 6:18
Galatians 6:9-10
Ephesians 2:10
Titus 3:14

36. Intentionality in Relationships
Old Testament:
Proverbs 27:9
Ecclesiastes 4:9-10
New Testament:
Romans 12:10
Colossians 3:12-14
Ephesians 4:32
1 Peter 4:8-10
Philippians 2:3-4
1 Thessalonians 5:11
Hebrews 10:24-25

37. Apologetics and Defense
Old Testament:
Isaiah 1:18
Psalm 119:46
New Testament:
1 Peter 3:15
Jude 1:3
Acts 17:2-3
2 Corinthians 10:5
Philippians 1:16
2 Timothy 4:2
Colossians 4:6

38. Building Trust and Reliability
Old Testament:
Proverbs 11:13
Psalm 15:2
New Testament:
Matthew 5:37
Luke 16:10
1 Corinthians 4:2
1 Thessalonians 5:24
Ephesians 4:25
2 Corinthians 8:21
Hebrews 13:18

39. Endurance in Trials
Old Testament:
Isaiah 40:31
Psalm 34:19
New Testament:
James 1:2-4
Romans 5:3-5
2 Timothy 2:3
1 Peter 1:6-7
Philippians 4:13
2 Corinthians 4:16-18
Hebrews 12:1-2

468 The Forge

40. Responding to Criticism
Old Testament:
- Proverbs 15:1
- Ecclesiastes 7:5

New Testament:
- Matthew 5:11-12
- James 1:19
- Romans 12:14
- 1 Peter 3:9
- 2 Timothy 2:24-25
- Titus 3:2
- Ephesians 4:31-32

41. Promoting Peace and Unity
Old Testament:
- Psalm 133:1
- Proverbs 12:20

New Testament:
- Romans 12:18
- Ephesians 4:3
- Colossians 3:15
- 1 Peter 3:8
- Philippians 2:2
- 1 Thessalonians 5:13
- James 3:17-18

42. Advocating for the Truth
Old Testament:
- Zechariah 8:16
- Proverbs 12:22

New Testament:
- John 8:31-32
- Ephesians 4:15
- 1 Timothy 6:12
- 2 Timothy 2:15
- 3 John 1:4
- Titus 1:9
- 1 Peter 3:15

43. Utilizing Spiritual Gifts
Old Testament:
- Exodus 31:3
- 1 Chronicles 29:14

New Testament:
- 1 Corinthians 12:4-7
- Romans 12:6-8
- Ephesians 4:11-12
- 1 Peter 4:10-11
- 1 Timothy 4:14
- 2 Timothy 1:6
- Colossians 3:23

44. Healthy Boundaries
Old Testament:
- Proverbs 25:17
- Nehemiah 2:17-20

New Testament:
- Galatians 6:5
- Matthew 5:37
- 2 Corinthians 6:14
- James 4:7
- Ephesians 5:11
- Romans 16:17
- 1 Corinthians 5:11

45. Living a Life of Worship
Old Testament:
- Psalm 95:6
- Isaiah 12:5

New Testament:
- Romans 12:1
- Colossians 3:16
- John 4:24
- Ephesians 5:19
- Hebrews 13:15
- Revelation 4:11
- Philippians 3:3

470 The Forge

46. Supporting Church Leadership
Old Testament:
Exodus 17:12
Numbers 11:17
New Testament:
1 Thessalonians 5:12-13
1 Timothy 5:17
Hebrews 13:17
1 Corinthians 16:16
1 Peter 5:2-3
Romans 12:8
Ephesians 4:11

47. Long-term Vision
Old Testament:
Proverbs 29:18
Isaiah 32:8
New Testament:
Philippians 3:13-14
Hebrews 12:1-2
Luke 14:28
2 Corinthians 4:18
Colossians 3:2
1 Peter 1:13
2 Timothy 4:7

48. Empathy and Compassion
Old Testament:
Psalm 103:13
Zechariah 7:9
New Testament:
Ephesians 4:32
Colossians 3:12
Romans 12:15
Philippians 2:4
1 Peter 3:8
2 Corinthians 1:3-4
James 2:13

49. Promoting Lifelong Learning
Old Testament:
>Proverbs 1:5
>Isaiah 1:17
New Testament:
>2 Timothy 2:15
>Colossians 1:10
>Romans 12:2
>Philippians 4:8-9
>2 Peter 3:18
>Hebrews 5:12-14
>Ephesians 4:13

50. Creating Safe Spaces
Old Testament:
>Psalm 46:1
>Isaiah 32:18
New Testament:
>Romans 15:7
>Galatians 6:2
>James 3:17
>1 Peter 5:7
>1 John 4:18
>Philippians 4:6-7
>Ephesians 4:2-3

51. Navigating Change
Old Testament:
>Ecclesiastes 3:1
>Isaiah 43:18-19
New Testament:
>Philippians 3:13-14
>2 Corinthians 5:17
>Romans 12:2
>Hebrews 13:8
>James 1:5
>Colossians 3:9-10
>1 Corinthians 9:22

The Forge

52. Faithfulness in Small Things
    Old Testament:
        Zechariah 4:10
        Proverbs 28:20
    New Testament:
        Luke 16:10
        Matthew 25:21
        Colossians 3:23
        1 Corinthians 4:2
        2 Timothy 2:2
        Galatians 6:9
        Revelation 2:10

About the Author

Dr. Chuck Carrington, PhD, EdS, MA, is a Christian therapist, educator, author, and speaker with over 30 years of experience working with couples, families, and individuals—  including trauma survivors, foster families and children, men recovering from pornography addiction, and the wives healing from betrayal trauma. He specializes in trauma, grief, and loss, with a focused practice in Christian counseling that emphasizes relational restoration in the wake of betrayal, infidelity, and emotional dysfunction.

Dr. Chuck's research explores innovative approaches to loss recovery, process addictions, betrayal trauma, post-traumatic embitterment, and the long-term impact of childhood family dysfunction. Blending biblical wisdom with evidence-based therapeutic models and a down-to-earth relational style, he brings compassion, clarity, and deep insight into how past wounds shape present relationships.

He is the founder of *Connect Christian Family Counseling*, where he walks alongside clients on their journey toward emotional and relational wholeness.

When he's not writing or counseling, Dr. Chuck enjoys reading, researching, leading workshops, and serving in local ministry projects. He also hosts free online support and discipleship groups. This book reflects his passion for bringing a practical, gospel-centered message to those navigating the complex challenges of modern life—helping them rediscover their identity and purpose in God's redemptive plan, and equipping them to grow in truth, strength, and grace.

Men's Leadership Devotional 475

If You Need Counseling or Help,

Dr Chuck offers Christian Faith-Based Counseling and Coaching in men's recovery from porn and cyber-addiction, Betrayal Trauma recovery for women, and restorative counseling to help heal and recover marriages after betrayal.

For a consultation via telehealth video, contact Dr Chuck to get more information on how to overcome the damage of betrayal and addiction. Use the website below to sign up for recovery and support groups, or to join Dr Chuck's online psychoeducational programs.

If you are looking for marriage enhancement counseling or coaching, Dr Chuck offers online webinars and forums to help Christian couples explore their marriage, and how it conforms to God's plan for marriage, to find forgiveness and healing, or to plan for an extraordinary marriage from the outset for engaged couples.

Believers should ask for the Faith-based community discount for the best possible pricing. Free groups include Healing Hearts for women damaged by betrayal, Overcomer's Group for men struggling with porn addiction and cyber addiction.

www.connectcounselor.com
Connect Christian Family Counseling
757 965-5450

Men's Leadership Devotional 477

Other Titles by Dr Chuck Carrington

Available on Amazon

Feelings Don't Care About Your Facts: How emotional Reasoning Hijacks Logic

We've all been there—trapped in an argument where logic and reason are rendered useless, where emotions drive the conversation, and no amount of evidence seems to matter. Emotional reasoning can wreak havoc on relationships, leaving partners feeling unheard, frustrated, and stuck in cycles of conflict.

The Renewed Mind: Rebuilding Trust in Marriage by Overcoming Porn Addiction for Life

Porn addiction is established long before its strong hold is realized, usually at some point in an adult relationship. This book takes science, counseling, and Christian living into a long term curative process. Included is information and direction on how to understand the impact of a man's porn addiction on his wife or partner, how to increase victim empathy, and the step to restoring her safety so trust can rebuild.

The Renewed Mind companion workbook

The Renewed Mind Study Guide, designed to complement the groundbreaking book The Renewed Mind: Rebuilding Trust in Marriage by Overcoming Porn Addiction for Life.

478 The Forge

The Loving Marriage: Jesus Reduce Me To Love. Lessons on living out 1 Corinthians in Marriage

Scripture provides a simple yet profound road map to guide all marriages on their journey of love, and in this book, we will help you develop a personal expression of love within your marriage, rooted in timeless biblical teachings.

The Masculine Edge: A Field Guide to Strength and Character

Discover the Edge You Were Born to Carry.
The Masculine Edge is a bold, honest, and deeply practical anthology for men who want more than surface-level faith.

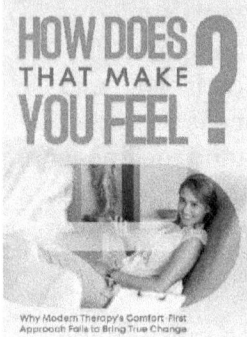

How Does That Make You Feel? Why Modern Therapy's Comfort-First Approach Fails to Bring True Change.

Not and anti-therapy book, but a candid insider's revelation on how modern therapy has become an enabling addiction to feelings over true recovery and health. Find the way back to healing, truth and what it really means to grow strong.

Check out Dr Chuck's **Seven Greatest Hits in Marriage Counseling**, a series of video supported coaching modules presenting his most effective tools to help couples exceed a typical marriage. At
www.connectcounselor.com
757 965-5450 DrChuck@connectcounselor.com

www.ingramcontent.com/pod-product-compliance
Lightning Source LLC
Chambersburg PA
CBHW070602230426
43670CB00010B/1381